HEBREWS:
DISPENSATIONALLY CONSIDERED

A GRACE EXPOSITIONAL COMMENTARY

SECOND EDITION

DR. DAVID ALAN GREENE

GraceWord Publishing, LLC
www.gracewordpublishing.com
U.S.A.

GRACEWORD PUBLISHING

Contents

To My Mother, A Saint Saved By Grace

And account that the longsuffering
of our Lord is salvation;
even as our beloved brother Paul also according to
the wisdom given unto him hath written unto you;
As also in all his epistles,
speaking in them of these things;
in which are some things hard to be understood,
which they that are unlearned and unstable wrest,
as they do also the other scriptures,
unto their own destruction.

– The Apostle Peter

x

Acknowledgements

To all who love God's Son, the Word of God, more than they love their customs and traditions. For they have put aside their traditions, customs, and religious beliefs and made the Word of God their sole authority. God will give you the understanding many seek, but few find.

I want to thank Jon and Susan McMahon for your encouragement. A special thank you to Greg Isaacs and Frances Greene who assisted me in the editing of this book.

Preface

In this preface, I would like to set your expectations. Think of an Air Traffic Controller speaking to a pilot who is bringing a plane in for landing. This pilot has never flown into this airport before. Applying the ATC's instructions, suddenly the runway appears and it is a perfect approach.

Hebrews can be a difficult book to understand. As with Air Traffic Controllers, following their instructions will help make your own approach line up with the purpose and intention of the author's letter to the Hebrews. I hope you find this information useful. This book approaches the subject from a dispensational view. If you are unfamiliar with this view, GraceWord published two books which explain what is called "systematic theology." They are referred to later in this book. This book is titled *Hebrews: Dispensationally Considered*.

I call myself a "plenary dispensationalist." This is different from the traditional view of the dispensations made popular by such men as Charles Ryrie and Lewis Sperry Chafer. I have great respect for both of them. The word "plenary" means "full, entire, and complete." Their views hold to several sequential dispensations or ages. This is different from the plenary view which holds that the Age of Grace is a parenthetical interruption to the Age of Law. The Age of Grace begins with the conversion of Paul and ends with the Rapture.

Following the Rapture, there remains seven years which are often referred to as the Seven Years of Tribulation. At its beginning, the Age of Law will resume. At the conclusion of these seven remaining years of the Age of Law, the Messiah will return as King for a great battle against Israel's enemies. Following this, the Millennial Reign will begin. Here, we cannot go into great detail for it is not the purpose of this book.

Therefore, everything from Moses to the conversion of Paul is the first part of the Age of Law. This includes the Gospels and the first part of the book of Acts! Jesus and His Twelve preached the Gospel of the Kingdom to Israel. (*cf.* Rom. 15:8.) Their message was Israel. It was about the fulfillment of God's promises –the coming Kingdom and their coming King.

Upon Paul's conversion, the Age of Grace began. He received the Gospel of Grace from the Risen Lord. He was chosen to be the Apostle to the Gentiles who was charged with carrying the Gospel of Grace. His gospel proclaimed salvation to the Gentiles by God's grace through faith without works. (*cf.* Eph. 2:8-9.) It was different from the Gospel of the Kingdom given to the Apostle Peter and the others. (*cf.* Gal. 2:7-9.)

The Rapture will mark the end the Age of Grace. Those who believed the Gospel of Grace will be "raptured" or "caught away." His Appearing in the air to call His own must not be confused with His Second Coming. His Appearing occurs at the beginning of the Tribulation. At this point, the Age of Law will resume for the remainder of the seven years. The Second Coming occurs at the end of the seven years. The Age of Grace is a parenthetical interruption (just like this comment) to the Age of Law. Remove the parenthetical interruption and the entire sentence still makes sense. Peter wrote this warning to the Jews. He mentions the people who will twist the writings of the Apostle Paul. 2 Peter 3:16:

> 16 **As also in all his [Paul's] epistles, speaking in them of these things; in which are some things hard to be un-**

derstood, <u>which they that are unlearned and unstable wrest, as they do also the other scriptures, unto their own destruction</u>.

The book of Hebrews and the seven other Hebrew Epistles that follow were written to Jews. These Jews followed then and will follow the Kingdom Gospel. Not grasping this fact will make the book of Hebrews confusing. In the above verse, the word "wrest" means "to twist, pull, or force" into saying what it does not. Friend, we must let the Bible speak, We must not force it to say something it does not.

Introduction

In Galatians 2, we find the agreement made between Paul and the other Apostles. They all agree that Peter and the others would take the Gospel of the Kingdom to the Jews called the "circumcision." While Paul, the Apostle to the Gentiles, would take the Gospel of Grace to the Gentiles called the "uncircumcision." Galatians 2:7-9:

> 7 But contrariwise, when they saw that <u>the gospel of the uncircumcision</u> was committed unto me, as <u>the gospel of the circumcision</u> was unto Peter; 8 (For he that wrought effectually in Peter to the apostleship of the circumcision, the same was mighty in me toward the Gentiles:)
>
> 9 And when James, Cephas, and John, who seemed to be pillars, perceived the grace that was given unto me, they gave to me and Barnabas the right hands of

fellowship; that <u>we should go unto the heathen</u>, and <u>they unto the circumcision</u>.

Rest assured. In no way does this minimize the Cross or God's singular work of His Son's death, burial, and resurrection. If you are saved by the Gospel of Grace you received your salvation as a gift from God by believing. For you, there is no requirement of works to either achieve your salvation or maintain it. You were bought by His blood . . . period.

Here is an important fact that Gentiles and those saved by grace through faith should know. Hebrews was not written to you! However, understanding its message will provide you with a deeper insight into Israel's current state and their future. This is only possible if it is understood from the right dispensational perspective. The Jews have a long history and bumpy relationship with God. The promises and prophecies He gave to them belong exclusively to the children of Israel. They cannot be rewritten or changed. They cannot be stolen by another religious group for whatever reason. God is faithful to fulfill His promises.

The rulers of Israel, as representatives of Israel, messed up big time when they crucified their

Messiah. Yet, God prophesied this would happen in Daniel 9:26. In Stephen's speech before the Sanhedrin, he charged these rulers with killing their Messiah. Their response was to drag him out of the city and stone him. It was at this point, we are first introduced to Saul. (*cf.* Acts 7:58.)

Israel's timeline was established in Daniel's prophecy. It helps to explain the temporary suspension when the Messiah was cut off. In Daniel 9, Daniel asked God a question, "When will You restore Jerusalem?" The answer he received far exceeded his expectations. This is explained in detail in my book *The Glorious Destiny of Israel – The Fulfillment of God's Promises and Prophecies to Israel.* Below, I will summarize it for you.

God gave Daniel a timeline: 490 years were determined for punishment for Israel. At the 483-year mark, the Messiah would be cutoff, but only for a while. Here we find the origin of the seven remaining years. These seven years are currently being held in abeyance until God finishes His work with the Gentiles. God sent Paul with the Gospel of Grace for the Gentiles. Upon the Rapture, with the removal of those saved by grace through faith, the clock for Daniel's timeline, having just seven remaining years, will resume. This is the Tribulation.

The prophecy points to a key point in time for the Jews. Again, this is about the Jews here. At the end of the seven remaining years, here is what God said will be completed. (*cf.* Dan. 9.) At the end of the 490 years, God promised:

- ✓ to finish the transgression,
- ✓ to make an end of sin,
- ✓ to forgive iniquity,
- ✓ to bring in everlasting righteousness,
- ✓ to seal up vision and prophet, and
- ✓ to anoint the most holy place.

So far, 483 of the 490 years have passed. The remaining seven years are being held in abeyance. Again, when the Age of Grace ends with the Rapture, the remaining seven years of the Age of Law will resume.

The Pauline letters were written to those saved by grace through faith. Hebrews is the first book to follow Paul's letters. All seven of the epistles that follow Hebrews were written to Jewish believers. These believers followed, are following, or will follow the Kingdom Gospel. Their purpose is to strengthen and encourage the Jewish believers especially as they go through the Tribulation to come.

In Hebrews, we see that the sins of the Jews are not forgiven until the return of their Messiah. Until then, their sins are held in "remission." It would be impossible to apply this to those saved by grace through faith! Grace Believers have already received forgiveness of their sins: past, present, and future. For greater details on this, consider reading my book *Letters To Theophilus – Are You Ready For The End Times?*

There is no doubt that Hebrews was written to those who follow the Kingdom Gospel. To be saved, they must acknowledge that Jesus Christ is the Messiah and He is the Son of God. They must repent and be baptized. After this, they are required to follow the Law. However, due to Israel's poor track record of continually losing faith, God added a requirement for them. They must continually prove their faith by their works or actions. As James wrote to them, "But wilt thou know, O vain man, that faith without works is dead?" (Jas. 2:20). This differentiates the Kingdom Gospel.

The authenticity of Hebrews has long passed questioning as it is included within the canon of Scripture. Some people question the authorship of this letter. I offer this in support of the Apostle Paul being its author. He had the training of a Pharisee. He knew both the Scriptures and the Jewish customs and traditions. In studying his other epistles, I continued to find similarities in the style. Most notably would be his method of presenting information and, then, he begins the next part with a conclusion prefaced by "therefore" or "wherefore."

The letter to the Hebrews was not signed. I believe that Paul did this intentionally. He did not want to cause confusion for the assemblies following the Gospel of Grace. Here is an interesting point. The Apostle Peter mentioned Paul in one of his letters. Peter's epistles were written to Jewish believers. His comments shed some light on the possible author of Hebrews. 2 Peter 3:14-15:

> 14 **Wherefore, beloved, seeing that ye look for such things, be diligent that ye may be found of him in peace, without spot, and blameless. 15 And account that the longsuffering of our Lord is salvation; <u>even as our beloved brother Paul also according to the wisdom given unto him hath written unto you</u>;**

Although this is not conclusive, I am personally comfortable believing that Paul wrote Hebrews.

I hope this information helps to provide the background you need. Whether agreed with or not, if you understand these points, your approach to reading this book will line up for a perfect landing.

1

Hebrews 1

We are moving forward with two suppositions. First, the letter was written by the Apostle Paul. Second, the letter was written to those who believe in the Gospel of the Kingdom and not those saved by grace through faith. The former holds to Jesus Christ being both their promised Messiah and the Son of God.

The Kingdom Gospel requires that they keep the Law. His apostles were to teaching followers to observe all the things which Jesus had commanded to do. (*cf.* Matt. 28:20.) These Kingdom Believers were going through a very difficult time at the time Hebrews was written. They were suffering persecution from both the religious Jews and the Roman authorities. However, the contents of this letter will be applied in the future by those faithful

Jews who will "endure" to the end. The Tribulation is actually a testing of true Israel who are distinguished by their "enduring" faith.

When the Bible uses the word "fathers" in connection with Israel, it is speaking of Abraham, Isaac, and Jacob. God said to Moses, ". . . I am the God of thy fathers, the God of Abraham, and the God of Isaac, and the God of Jacob . . ." (Acts 7:32). We find this same reference at the opening of this letter. Hebrews 1:1:

> 1 **God, who at sundry times and in divers manners spake in time past <u>unto the fathers</u> by the prophets,**

God chose various men who He ordained to speak on his behalf. These prophets were His representatives and were authenticated by miracles, signs, and wonders. We have only to look at the Old Testament to find titles of books named after these prophets of God.

More recently, God chose to speak to Israel through His Son. There is a verse in Romans that has troubled more than one Bible teacher. Paul makes a statement that only makes sense if it is interpreted literally and dispensationally. He is explaining to the Gentiles why the Messiah came. Romans 15:8:

2

8 Now I say that <u>Jesus Christ was a</u> <u>minister of the circumcision</u> for the truth of God, <u>to confirm the promises</u> <u>made unto the fathers</u>:

Again, the word "circumcision" refers to the Jews who bore a physical mark as members of the Abrahamic Covenant.

We continue speaking about God. Hebrews 1:2-3:

2 Hath in these last days <u>spoken unto us</u> <u>by his Son</u>, whom he hath appointed heir of all things, by whom also he made the worlds;

3 Who being the brightness of his glory, and the express image of his person, and upholding all things by the word of his power, when he had by himself purged our sins, sat down on the right hand of the Majesty on high;

He is speaking of Jesus Christ Who was involved in the Creation. Paul wrote in Colossians 1:15-17:

15 Who is the image of the invisible God, the firstborn of every creature:

16 For by him were all things created, that are in heaven, and that are in earth, visible and invisible, whether they be thrones, or dominions, or principalities, or powers: all things were created by him, and for him: **17** And he is before all things, and by him all things consist.

God was present in Jesus Christ during His earthly ministry to the Jews. He acted as God's representative and spoke to the Jews on God's behalf.

Did you know the role of Messiah has three offices? They are: Prophet, Priest, and King. Prophets do not speak on their own behalf, but speaks the words given to them by God. While on earth Christ fulfilled the office of Prophet by speaking not for Himself, but the words He received from the Father. John 12:49-50:

49 For I have not spoken of myself; but the Father which sent me, he gave me a commandment, what I should say, and what I should speak. **50** And I know that his commandment is life everlasting: whatsoever I speak therefore, even as the Father said unto me, so I speak.

In the book of Hebrews, we will witness the second office of Priest. The third and final office of the Messiah is King. It will not be until the end when as King He will return to defend His people Israel and be victorious over their enemies.

Paul goes on to compare Jesus Christ's unique position to the angels who are God's messengers. Verses 4-5:

> 4 **Being made so much better than the angels, as he hath by inheritance obtained a more excellent name than they.**
>
> 5 **For unto which of the angels said he at any time, Thou art my Son, this day have I begotten thee? And again, I will be to him a Father, and he shall be to me a Son?**

The above words refer to the Father and Son's unique relationship. These words are quoting Psalms 2:7. God tells King David about the future of his kingdom and how He will establish an eternal kingdom on David's throne. 2 Samuel 7:12-16:

> 12 **And when thy days be fulfilled, and thou shalt sleep with thy fathers, I will**

set up thy seed after thee, which shall proceed out of thy bowels, and I will establish his kingdom.

13 He shall build an house for my name, and I will stablish the throne of his kingdom forever.

14 I will be his father, and he shall be my son. If he commit iniquity, I will chasten him with the rod of men, and with the stripes of the children of men:

15 But my mercy shall not depart away from him, as I took it from Saul, whom I put away before thee.

16 And thine house and thy kingdom shall be established for ever before thee: thy throne shall be established forever.

The book of Hebrews speaks to those to whom the promise was made: King David and his descendant, Jesus Christ.

In the following verse, there is a word that is often misused. The Bible refers to Jesus Christ as being the "first begotten." This is significant. It means the first one to be resurrected or made live again from the dead. The only One Who is born-again is Jesus Christ Who is the first to be raised to life from the dead. Hebrews 1:6-8:

> **6 And again, when he bringeth in the firstbegotten into the world, he saith, And let all the angels of God worship him.**
>
> **7 And of the angels he saith, Who maketh his angels spirits, and his ministers a flame of fire.**
>
> **8 But unto the Son he saith, Thy throne, O God, is for ever and ever: a sceptre of righteousness is the sceptre of thy kingdom.**

Let's compare the above to what the Apostle John wrote to the Jews who persevere to the end. Revelation 1:5:

> **5 And from Jesus Christ, who is the faithful witness, and <u>the first begotten of the dead</u>, and the prince of the kings of the earth . . .**

The following specifically applies to the Righteous

One. Hebrews 1:9-12:

9 Thou hast loved righteousness, and hated iniquity; therefore God, even [that is to say] thy God, hath anointed thee with the oil of gladness above thy fellows.

10 And, Thou, Lord, in the beginning hast laid the foundation of the earth; and the heavens are the works of thine hands:

11 They shall perish; but thou remainest; and they all shall wax [grow] old as doth [does] a garment;

12 And as a vesture shalt thou fold them up, and they shall be changed: but thou art the same, and thy years shall not fail.

As Creation grows old like clothing, God the Creator does not change. He will always remain the same.

The Creator has never said to the angels what He has said to His Son. Verse 13:

13 But to which of the angels said he at any time, Sit on my right hand, until I

make thine enemies thy footstool?

This comes from King David who made a statement concerning both the LORD, Elohim, and the Lord, Adonai. These names identify the Father and Son respectively. Psalm 110:1:

> 1 **The LORD said unto my Lord,**
> **Sit thou at my right hand,**
> **until I make thine enemies thy**
> **footstool.**

Paul continues to speak about angels and includes their purpose. Hebrews 1:14:

> 14 **Are they not all ministering spirits,**
> **sent forth to minister for them who**
> **shall be heirs of salvation?**

The true children of God are His heirs. Angels act as His servants and for the benefit of the heirs of salvation. Remember, the inheritance will be received in the future.

2

Hebrews 2

With the number of references made in this chapter, we can clearly see this letter was written to Jewish believers. Those who are followers of the Kingdom Gospel had received it from their Messiah or the Twelve. As we move deeper into the book of Hebrews, we will see more evidence that his book was not written to those saved by grace through faith.

The word "heed" means "to be mindful of; to regard with care; to take notice of; to attend to; to observe." Hebrews 2:1:

> 1 **Therefore we ought to give the more earnest heed to the things which we have heard, lest at any time we should let them slip.**

Letting this slip from memory could be fatal could be fatal to their salvation. Their faith must be continually proven by works and those who ". . . shall endure unto the end, the same shall be saved" (Matt. 24:13). You may recall the final earthly meeting the Lord had with His disciples before His ascension. There, He instructed them. Matthew 28:20:

> 20 **Teaching them <u>to observe all things whatsoever I have commanded you</u>: and, lo, I am with you alway, even unto the end of the world. Amen.**

In the case of "observing" the Law, it means keeping the Law, following the Law, or doing the requirements of the Law.

Paul continues to urge them to keep the Law. Remember, for the Jews, breaking or failing to observe the Law has consequences. The word "stedfast" means "firmly fixed or established." Hebrews 2:2-4:

> 2 **For if the word spoken by angels was stedfast, and <u>every transgression and disobedience received a just recompence of reward</u>;**

3 How shall we escape, if we neglect so great salvation; which at <u>the first began to be spoken by the Lord</u>, and was confirmed unto us by them that heard him;

4 God also bearing them witness, both with signs and wonders, and with divers miracles, and gifts of the Holy Ghost, according to his own will?

Notice that it was the Lord Who first gave the Jews the Jews the Gospel of Grace and it was confirmed "by them that heard Him." These are the same disciples Jesus commanded to teach them ". . . to observe all things whatsoever I have commanded you" (Matt. 28:20). The Jews expected miracles, signs, and wonders from those who brought them the word of God. Once validated, they were to obey it.

Paul alludes to Israel's future role in God's restored Creation. Verse 5:

5 For unto the angels hath he not put in subjection <u>the world to come</u>, whereof we speak.

We read in Genesis that God gave Adam authority

to manage His Creation. Genesis 1:26:

> 26 And God said, Let us make man in our image, after our likeness: and let them have dominion over the fish of the sea, and over the fowl of the air, and over the cattle, and over all the earth, and over every creeping thing that creepeth upon the earth.

Now, Paul quotes the words written by King David in Psalms 8:4-6 where he speaks about the creation of man and his fall. God gave Adam dominion over the earth. Keeping this in mind, Paul continues with verses Hebrews 2:6-8:

> 6 But one in a certain place testified, saying, What is man, that thou art mindful of him? or the son of man, that thou visitest him?

> 7 Thou madest him a little lower than the angels; thou crownedst him with glory and honour, and didst set him over the works of thy hands:

> 8 Thou hast put all things in subjection under his feet. For in that he put all in subjection under him, he left nothing

**that is not put under him. But now we
see not yet all things put under him.**

What caused this authority to be removed? It was original sin. The penalty for sin is death and through our first parents, the curse of death was placed upon all. That authority given to Adam to rule the earth will be given to a Man again. That Man is related to Adam, Abraham, and King David. That Man is Jesus Christ.

Notice the next verse. It begins with the word "but" which contrasts the following with the previous. Jesus Christ was the Man who suffered death, however He was righteous before God. Death had no hold over Him. Therefore, God raised Him from the dead and crowned with glory and honor. Verse 9:

> 9 **But we see Jesus, who was made a little lower than the angels for the suffering of death, crowned with glory and honour; that he by the grace of God should taste death for every man.**

God arranged this in advance for a purpose. Verse 10:

> 10 **For it became him, for whom are all**

things, and by whom are all things, in <u>bringing many sons unto glory</u>, to make <u>the captain of their salvation</u> perfect through sufferings.

Jesus Christ was referred to by the prophet Isaiah as the Suffering Servant. (I recommend that you stop for a moment and read Isa. 42:1-4, 49:1-6, 50:4-11, and 52:13-53:12.) It was through Christ's suffering that His brethren, the children of Abraham, will be saved. Verses 11-13:

11 **For both he that sanctifieth and they who are sanctified are all of one: for which cause he is not ashamed to call them <u>brethren</u>,**

12 **Saying, I will declare thy name unto my brethren, in the midst of the church [assembly] will I sing praise unto thee.**

13 **And again, I will put my trust in him. And again, Behold I and the children which God hath given me.**

It speaks of Him Who sanctifies and those who are sanctified as being one. Christ is the Son of Abraham and, like all the children of Abraham, they are brethren or brothers. The Apostle John wrote this

16

concerning the Messiah, "He was in the world, and the world was made by him, and the world did not accept him. <u>He came unto his own, and his own received him not</u>" (Jn. 1:10-11).

Remember, the Messiah and the other children of Abraham are both of the same flesh and blood. They are of the same family. This allowed Jesus Christ to be the substitute for His brethren. This is called substitutionary atonement as someone else pays the penalty to redeems another. There are specific Jewish rite for this. The Jewish concept is called "the kinsman-redeemer" where the word "redeemer" means "one who buys back." There are three rules to qualify this kinsman-redeemer. First, the kinsman-redeemer must be a close relative to the distressed person. Second, the kinsman-redeemer must be willing to pay the redemption price to regain the lost property or person. Finally, the kinsman-redeemer must have the ability or power to pay the redemption price. (See Lev. 25:25-26; Ruth 2:1, 2:20, 3:11-13.) So, who is holding these debtors captive? We find out who this culprit is in verse 14:

> 14 **Forasmuch then as the children are partakers of flesh and blood, he also himself likewise took part of the same; that through death he might destroy <u>him that had the power of death, that is,</u>**

<u>the devil;</u>

Satan holds the power of death. He is the prosecutor and holds those accountable who broke God's Law. Satan brings charges for breaking the Law before the righteous God. Being righteous, God has no choice but to keep His Word. Paul teaching that life cannot come from the Law; only condemnation. However, if there is a kinsman-redeemer who meets the qualifications, then the debt can be paid on someone else's behalf.

Jesus Christ, Son of God and Son of Abraham, met the qualifications of the kinsman-redeemer. He accomplished for His brethren what Israel could not accomplish for themselves. Verses 15-16:

> 15 **And deliver them who through fear of death were all their lifetime subject to bondage.**
>
> 16 **For verily he took not on him the nature of angels; but he took on him the seed of Abraham.**

Their lifetime of fear refers to the bondage of the Law. Jesus tried to make this fact plain. Yet, while their Messiah was with them, the religious Jews refuted Him. Notice their response in John 8:33-36:

33 They answered him, We be Abraham's seed, and were never in bondage to any man: how sayest thou, Ye shall be made free? **34** Jesus answered them, Verily, verily, I say unto you, Whosoever committeth sin is the servant of sin.

35 And the servant abideth not in the house for ever: but the Son abideth ever. **36** If the Son therefore shall make you free, ye shall be free indeed.

Here is an important point concerning the Law. The Jews were required and still are required today to keep *all* the Law. As we begin to understand the weight of the Law upon the Jews, we can understand the meaning of bondage.

The children of Israel made a contractual agreement with God. This is still a binding agreement. If they keep their part of the agreement, then God would bless them. If they broke even one point of that agreement, then God would curse them. In the Wilderness, God presented Israel with the Mosaic Covenant. This contractual agreement was ratified – agreed to or accepted – by Israel. They became eternally bound to it and God would be the Overseer of this agreement. Exodus 19:7-8:

7 And Moses came and called for the elders of the people, and laid before their faces all these words which the LORD commanded him.

8 And all the people answered together, and said, <u>All that the LORD hath spoken we will do</u>. And Moses returned the words of the people unto the LORD.

Did you see the "all" in the above? Most Christians and some Jews are unaware of the consequences of breaking the Mosaic Covenant simply referred to as "the Law."

In the following, we have a concise summary of what took place the day Israel bound themselves to that Covenant. The conditions of that agreement are often referred to as "the blessings and curses." Deuteronomy 30:15-20:

15 See, I have set before thee this day life and good, and death and evil;

16 In that I command thee this day to love the LORD thy God, to walk in his ways, and to keep his commandments and his statutes and his judgments, that thou mayest live and multiply: and the

LORD thy God shall bless thee in the land whither thou goest to possess it.

17 But if thine heart turn away, so that thou wilt not hear, but shalt be drawn away, and worship other gods, and serve them; 18 I denounce unto you this day, that ye shall surely perish, and that ye shall not prolong your days upon the land, whither thou passest over Jordan to go to possess it.

19 I call heaven and earth to record this day against you, that I have set before you life and death, blessing and cursing: therefore choose life, that both thou and thy seed may live:

20 That thou mayest love the LORD thy God, and that thou mayest obey his voice, and that thou mayest cleave unto him: for he is thy life, and the length of thy days: that thou mayest dwell in the land which the LORD sware unto thy fathers, to Abraham, to Isaac, and to Jacob, to give them.

There is one more point I need to make before we move on. It concerns the "bondage" of the Law which remains a great weight upon the Jewish people. The Apostle James summarized it best. Writing to the Jews, he tells them if they strive to keep the Law and fail in one small detail, then they have failed completely. James 2:10:

> 10 **For whosoever shall keep the whole law, and yet offend in one point, he is guilty of all.**

Great news for the children of Israel, their Kinsman-Redeemer is able to make their redemption because He did not fail! He kept the entire Law during His time on earth. Therefore, He is able to do for them what they cannot do for themselves.

In the following, the word "behoved" means that "it was necessary for." Therefore, it was necessary for Jesus Christ to be made like his brethren. The reason for this was explained above. Hebrews 2:17:

> 17 **Wherefore in all things it behoved him to be made like unto his brethren, <u>that he might be a merciful and faithful high priest in things pertaining to God,</u> to make reconciliation for the sins of the people.**

These verses can only be applied to the Jews – His brethren – who are the children of Israel. Jesus Christ is able to make restitution and redemption on their behalf as their Kinsman-Redeemer.

In the next verse, the word "succour" means "to provide help, aid, or relief" to someone in need. In this case, the aid is being provided to those who are under the Law and are tempted to break it. Verse 18:

> 18 **For in that he himself hath suffered being tempted, he is able to succour them that are tempted.**

This is an important point. The redemption spoken of in Hebrews 2 can only be applied to the children of Abraham. It is because Jesus Christ is the Son of Abraham. We see this in the very first verse in the New Testament. Matthew 1:1:

> 1 **The book of the generation of Jesus Christ, the son of David, the son of Abraham.**

Jesus Christ is the Son of Abraham. He is able to buy back or redeem the lost children of Abraham. Look at two verses. Jesus directs His Twelve in Matthew 10:6:

6 But go rather to <u>the lost sheep of the house of Israel.</u>

Again, we see it in Matthew 15:24:

24 But he answered and said, I am not sent but [only] unto <u>the lost sheep of the house of Israel</u>.

Jesus Christ is the Kinsman-Redeemer Who is able and willing to redeem His brethren.

3

Hebrews 3

As we read further along, it becomes more difficult to interpret this letter as being sent to anyone else other than the Jews. There can be to forcing it to apply to another unrelated party. We cannot suddenly and in mid-stream jump into another boat and say this now applies to "the church." That would be misinterpreting God's Word. Those who do ". . . are unlearned and unstable wrest" or twist the Word of God, ". . . unto their own destruction." (*cf.* 2 Pet. 3:16.) Therefore, this letter continues with its message to the children of Israel and no one else.

The word "holy" is sometimes misinterpreted as meaning "perfect." However, that is incorrect. The word "holy" means "separated or set a part." Moses recorded God's words to Israel in Leviticus 11:45:

45 For I am the LORD that bringeth you up out of the land of Egypt, to be your God: <u>ye shall therefore be holy, for I am holy</u>.

He is not saying being perfect as God is perfect. He is saying be separated from the world as God is separated from the word. We see these words again when the Apostle Peter writes to the Jews in 1 Peter 1:16:

16 Because it is written, <u>Be ye holy; for I am holy</u>.

Israel must remain separated from the world because of God's specific purpose for them. God called Israel out from all the other nations. God chose one special people for Himself.

In view of the above, Paul addresses Israel appropriately in Hebrews 3:1:

1 Wherefore, holy brethren, partakers of the heavenly calling, consider the Apostle and High Priest of our profession, Christ Jesus;

Let us look at two titles used to describe Jesus Christ. The first is Apostle. An "apostle" is "someone sent on a mission as a representative of someone else." An apostle carries a message on behalf of another. This describes the role of Jesus during His earthly ministry. He carried the words the Father had given him to the Jews. The second title is Priest. A "priest" is someone who "intercedes on behalf of someone in their relationship with God."

Those who are saved by grace through faith are justified immediately. Each of them is proclaimed "not guilty" for all sins: past, present, and future. None of them needs a priest to intercede on their behalf as they had the righteousness of Christ imputed to them. Spiritually, they are in Christ. There is no need for an intercessor as they can approach God directly.

Paul tells true Israel that their High Priest remains faithful to the One Who appointed Him. He was given a role that no other priest could possibly equal. Paul compared Christ with Moses. Moses is called a "type" or "example" that fore-shadows the future. Verses 2-5:

> 2 Who was faithful to him [God] that appointed him, as also Moses was faithful in all his house.

> 3 For this man [Jesus Christ] was count-

ed worthy of more glory than Moses, inasmuch as he who hath builded the house hath more honour than the house.

4 For every house is builded by some man; but he that built all things is God.

5 And Moses verily was faithful in all his house, as a servant, for a testimony of those things which were to be spoken after;

Moses was a faithful servant and a "type" or testimony of the One to come. He laid the groundwork for Jesus Christ. Moses knew this as he humbly fulfilled his duties.

Continuing with his comparison, Paul describes Christ's "house" applies to Israel. Unlike the Gospel of Grace, there is a condition. Mentioned before, it is now mentioned again! The conditional statement begins with the word "if" in verse 6:

6 But Christ as a son over his own house; whose house are we, <u>if we hold fast the confidence and the rejoicing of the hope firm unto the end.</u>

Do not overlook this critical point: there is a condition for the Jews' salvation. They must "hold fast" to their faith until the end! This faith must be continually proven. Again, remember Jesus' words to His disciples. Those who ". . . shall endure unto the end, the same shall be saved" (Matt. 24:13).

The word "provocation" means "anything that excites anger or causes resentment." Below, we have a comparison with something that happened while Israel was in the Wilderness. They provoked God's wrath. Verses 7-10:

> 7 **Wherefore (as the Holy Ghost saith, Today if ye will hear his voice,** 8 <u>**Harden not your hearts, as in the provocation, in the day of temptation in the wilderness:**</u>
>
> 9 **When your fathers tempted me, proved me, and saw my works forty years.**
>
> 10 **Wherefore I was grieved with that generation, and said, They do alway err in their heart; and they have not known my ways.** 11 **So I sware [swore] in my wrath, They shall not enter into my rest.)**

With Moses, Israel tested God's patience. They provoked God and it resulted in an additional forty years in the Wilderness. That generation all died. They were prevented from entering the Promised Land which is a "type" for the coming Eternal Kingdom.

Paul urges them to "take heed" which means "to pay attention to, listen to, and consider well." The history of the Jews was filled with unbelief or lack of faith. Therefore, God is dealing with this issue by requiring they continually maintain their faith with hope and actions as proof. Notice that Paul addresses them as "brethren." Verses 12-13:

> 12 Take heed, brethren, lest there be in any of you <u>an evil heart of unbelief</u>, in <u>departing from the living God.</u>

> 13 But exhort one another daily, while it is called To day; lest any of you be hardened through the deceitfulness of sin.

Unbelief is the same as "departing from the living God." There is no salvation apart from trusting God and believing in His Word.

There is something different here. Salvation for

those saved by grace through faith believe, once they are saved, is eternally secure. However, Israel's long history in which they lacked faith has brought them to a different place. As such, God is dealing with them another way as we see in verses 14-15:

> 14 **For we are made partakers of Christ,** <u>**if we hold the beginning of our confidence [faith] stedfast unto the end;**</u>
>
> 15 **While it is said, Today if ye will hear his voice,** <u>**harden not your hearts**</u>**, as in the provocation.**

Paul describes what he meant by "the provocation" in verse 8 above. There is no doubt that this can only apply to Israel. The comparison is completed by concluding the sin of Israel was their unbelief. Verses 16-18:

> 16 **For some, when they had heard, did provoke: howbeit [because of this] not all that came out of Egypt by Moses.**
>
> 17 **But with whom was he grieved forty years? was it not with them that had sinned, whose carcases fell in the wilderness?**

18 And to whom sware [swore] he that they should not enter into his rest, but to them that believed not?

Israel continually lost their faith and turned away from God. This, their salvation is conditional. They will not receive salvation through works, but their works are proof of their continuing faith. Remember, this only applies to Israel and their Gospel of the Kingdom. Verse 19:

19 So we see that <u>they could not enter in because of unbelief.</u>

In the Wilderness, Israel abandoned God. As a result, that generation was not allowed to enter into the Promised Land. Simply put, It was due to their unbelief – their lack of faith.

4

Hebrews 4

Now that we are beginning Hebrews 4, is there any question in your mind this letter was written to Jews following the Kingdom Gospel? It becomes more and more difficult to interpret the context to apply to anyone other than the children of Israel. Those saved by the Gospel of Grace have eternal security in their salvation. Paul begins with a conclusion for his readers. They should fear! What!?! They should fear that they may lose out on their promise. Hebrews 4:1:

> 1 **Let us therefore fear,** lest, a promise being left us of entering into his rest, any of you should seem to come short of it.

God's promise to Israel is contingent upon

them maintaining faith and proving it by their actions. Therefore, what could cause them to lose out on this promise? Verse 2:

> 2 **For unto us was the gospel preached, as well as unto them: but the word preached did not profit them, not being mixed with faith in them that heard it.**

The Gospel of the Kingdom was preached to those who heard and believed through faith. But, to those who did not receive it in faith, it did not profit or do them any good. Why? This is because when they heard the gospel message it was not mixed or received by faith!

Pay close attention. We are going to see how faithful Israel, who must endure to the end, will be saved. As you know, "In the beginning God created the heaven and the earth" (Gen. 1:1). Creation took Him six days. See what God tells us about what happened next. Genesis 2:1-3:

> 1 **Thus the heavens and the earth were finished, and all the host of them.** 2 **And on the seventh day God ended his work which he had made; and he rested on the seventh day from all his work which he had made.**

3 And God blessed the seventh day, and sanctified it: because that in it he had rested from all his work which God created and made.

Today, Jews still celebrate the Sabbath to honor the day God rested. In the book, *The Glorious Destiny of Israel,* I look at God's recreation or restoration of His Creation in seven ages. This is seen through the eyes of the Jews. The seventh age is called the Eternal Sabbath. What does that have to do with Israel's salvation?

Paul addressed the faithful Jews who wait by faith in the hope for the promise of the eternal kingdom. This eternal kingdom is often referred to as God's "sabbath" or "eternal rest." Hebrews 4:3-4:

3 For we which [who] have believed do enter into rest, as he said, As I have sworn in my wrath, if they shall enter into my rest: although the works were finished from the foundation of the world. 4 For he spake in a certain place of [concerning] the seventh day on this wise [way], And <u>God did rest the seventh day from all his works</u>.

Salvation for the Gentiles was a mystery hidden in God from before the world. That is until it was revealed to the Apostle Paul. There is no place in the Bible that disclosed God's offer of salvation to the Gentiles prior to Paul. 1 Corinthians 2:7-8:

> **7 But we speak the wisdom of God in <u>a</u> <u>mystery</u>, even <u>the hidden wisdom</u>, which God ordained before the world unto our glory: 8 Which none of the princes of this world knew: for had they known it, they would not have crucified the Lord of glory.**

Had the powers, principalities, and rulers of darkness known this, they would not have crucified God's Son thereby sealing their doom.

God knew what they would do to His Son. He had a contingency plan for the Jews' salvation because He knew they would fail. For the Jews, all His plans were disclosed by the Hebrew prophets. Let us look at one of the major Old Testament prophets: Jeremiah. This shows God's great love for the fathers of His people Israel. It is worth reading. Jeremiah 31:31-32:

> **31 Behold, the days come, saith the LORD, that <u>I will make a new covenant</u>**

with the house of Israel, and with the house of Judah:

32 Not according to the covenant that I made with their fathers in the day that I took them by the hand to bring them out of the land of Egypt; which my covenant they brake, although I was an husband unto them, saith the LORD:

I am sure you have heard of the "new covenant." Christ disclosed this new covenant on the last night He was with His disciples. It is commonly referred to as Communion. God explains the purpose of this new covenant. It has to do with Israel's future. Verse 33:

33 But this shall be the covenant that I will make with the house of Israel; After those days, saith the LORD, I will put my law in their inward parts, and write it in their hearts; and will be their God, and they shall be my people.

As He continues to explain, we realize He is speaking of the end times. For those of you familiar with the prophecy in Daniel 9, the following confirms it. Verse 34:

34 And they shall teach no more every man his neighbour, and every man his brother, saying, Know the LORD: for they shall all know me, from the least of them unto the greatest of them, saith the LORD: for <u>I will forgive their iniquity</u>, and <u>I will remember their sin no more</u>.

Note the future tense of the verbs are used: "I will forgive" and "I will remember." That makes this a prophecy of something that will come to pass. Israel has God's Word on this. This is addressed in greater detail in the book *The Glorious Destiny of Israel.*

Reading the book of Hebrews is not for the novice or faint of heart. It takes time and thought. For this reason, we are going slow and providing plenty of supporting detail. There are two things I would like you to see clearly. First, the book of Hebrews was unquestionably written to believing Jews. They heard and believed the Gospel of the Kingdom. They are called "the remnant" or "true Israel." Second, I would like you to see how it all ties together. From the Old Testament prophecies, the four Gospels, Hebrews, the seven Hebrew epistles and the book of Revelation. It may seem difficult because this is rarely, if ever, taught in churches today. If you have never heard this, it does not mean that it is not true!

It is time to return to the original text. Hebrews 3:4-5:

> **4 For he spake in a certain place of the seventh day on this wise, And <u>God did rest the seventh day from all his works</u>.**
>
> **5 And in this place again, If they shall enter into my rest.**

The wonderful news is for true Israel – those who hold onto the hope by faith to the Kingdom Gospel and endure to the end. They will experience and enjoy the peace of the Eternal Sabbath to come. This is not one day, but an eternity of peace and rest.

This future event was promised to King David and later confirmed by the Prophet Daniel. It is the hope of this event that the Jews must hold onto by faith. This Kingdom was promised to King David concerning his throne and his Descendent who would reign forever. Jesus is called the Son of David for a reason. The Jews who knew about this promise recognized Him. For that reason, the crowds shouted "Son of David" as He entered Jerusalem. Those who first heard the Gospel of the Kingdom believed. Paul warns those who believed that they should not harden their hearts which means lose that faith. Verses 6-7:

6 Seeing therefore it remaineth that some must enter therein, and they to whom it was first preached entered not in because of unbelief:

7 Again, he limiteth a certain day, saying in [to] David, To day, after so long a time; as it is said, To day if ye will hear his voice, harden not your hearts.

The arrival of the Kingdom and the crowning of eternal King still remain in the future. As sure as God is faithful, it will happen as He promised.

Paul argues: If those who heard and believed the gospel already had received the eternal rest, then there would have been no need for Jesus to speak about another day in the future. Verses 8-9:

8 For if Jesus had given them rest, then would he not afterward have spoken of another day. **9** There remaineth therefore a rest to the people of God.

Those who enter into His rest will not need to work. However, for the Jews, their faith requires works as proof. James, writing to the same Jews, wrote this. James 2:26:

26 For as the body without the spirit is dead, <u>so faith without works is dead</u> also.

Many churches erroneously merge the above verse with salvation by grace through faith preached by Paul in Ephesians 2:8-9. For those who know their Bible rightly divided, it should trip a circuit breaker. Yet, a lot of churches today do it!

The Eternal Sabbath of Israel still remains in the future. It will happen when their Messiah returns to establish His eternal Kingdom. Then, and only then, will their eternal rest begin.[1] Hebrews 3:10:

10 For he that is entered into his rest, he also hath ceased from his own works, as God did from his.

There will be no easing up on the works requirement for the Jews. Their salvation will come by faith – in believing what God said. They must believe in His Word. However, based upon their past, the Jews' faith must be continually tested or proven. As mentioned before, this is quite different from the Gospel of Grace. They are saved by grace through faith without works. The Gentiles' faith is not based

---

[1] Again, explained in detail in *The Glorious Destiny of Israel*.

upon sight, but based solely upon trusting God's Word. Paul wrote to the Gentiles, "For we walk by faith, not by sight" (2 Cor. 5:7).

The Jews who choose to follow the Gospel of the Kingdom must labor and prove their faith to earn their rest. Verse 11:

> 11 **Let us labour therefore to enter into that rest, lest any man fall after the same example of unbelief.**

The word "quick" means "living." Verse 12:

> 12 **For the word of God is quick, and powerful, and sharper than any two-edged sword, piercing even to the dividing asunder of soul and spirit, and of the joints and marrow, and is a discerner of the thoughts and intents of the heart.**

Jesus Christ knows "the thoughts and intents of the heart" of every individual that ever lived. There is no hiding or subterfuge with Him. It is foolishness to try. The word "manifest" means "made known." Verse 13:

> 3 **Neither is there any creature that is**

not manifest in his sight: but all things are naked and opened unto the eyes of him with whom we have to do.

The One Who is being described stands as the High Priest of those Jews who seek after the good news of the Kingdom. As their priest, He stands between them and a holy and just God. Verses 14-15:

> 14 Seeing then that <u>we have a great high priest</u>, that is passed into the heavens, <u>Jesus the Son of God</u>, let us hold fast our profession [of faith].
>
> 15 For we have not an high priest which cannot be touched with the feeling of our infirmities; but was in all points tempted like as we are, yet without sin.

He tells them that they have a High Priest Who was tempted as they are, but He never sinned. There-fore, their High Priest knows the feelings of their weaknesses.

He concludes with these encouraging words. The can be confident knowing Who their High Priest is and His ability to understand them. They may regularly come before the throne of God according to their needs. Verse 16:

16 Let us therefore come boldly unto the throne of grace, that we may obtain mercy, and find grace to help in time of need.

5

Hebrews 5

This chapter is about the Levitical priesthood which was established along with the Mosaic Covenant. This makes sense because the Jews are still under the Mosaic Law. Unlike those saved by grace through faith, the Jews remain under the Law. Notice what Jesus said concerning the Law and His own relationship to it. Matthew 5:17:

> **17 Think not that <u>I am come to destroy the law, or the prophets: I am not come to destroy, but to fulfil</u>.**

Then, He continued by referring to the end when the new heaven and earth are established. Verse 18:

> **18 For verily I say unto you, Till heaven and earth pass, one jot or one tittle shall**

in no wise pass from the law, till all be fulfilled.

So, for the Jews, the Law remains in effect. Their Messiah, in His life and death, fulfilled the Law. He is their Kinsman-Redeemer. As such, He is more than capable to redeem them through His sacrifice as their High Priest.

Paul starts by giving some history concerning the office of High Priest and its function as originally intended by God. Originally, the High Priest was chosen from among the brethren. Hebrew 5:1-3:

> 1 **For every high priest taken from among men is ordained for men in things pertaining to God, that he may offer both gifts and sacrifices for sins:**
>
> 2 **Who can have compassion on the ignorant, and on them that are out of the way; for that he himself also is compassed with infirmity.**
>
> 3 **And by reason hereof he ought, as for the people, so also for himself, to offer for sins.**

The High Priest, from the beginning, were men who

offered sacrifices not only for the people but also for themselves.

No one could choose to take this office. They were ordained by God. Aaron, the brother of Moses, was ordained by God as the first Levitical priest. He was the founder of the Levitical priesthood. Verse 4:

> 4 And no man taketh this honour unto himself, but he that is called of God, as was Aaron.

The High Priest was responsible for performing sacred duties of making sacrificial offerings to God on behalf of the people. He was the only one allowed to enter the Most Holy Place within the Temple. There, He would appear before the Judgment Seat of God only once a year. This would be done on the Day of Atonement called Yom Kippur.

Paul now compares this with Christ. He did not appoint Himself as High Priest. He was appointed by God His Father. Verse 5:

> 5 So also Christ glorified not himself to be made an high priest; but he that said unto him, Thou art my Son, to day have I begotten thee.

In the book of Genesis, we find a person of interest. His name is only mentioned twice in the Old Testament. The first time is in Genesis and second in Psalms. However, his name is mentioned nine times in the book of Hebrews under a slightly different spelling. Before we continue with Hebrews, let us look at the verses from the Old Testament. In each of these, can we find any similarities with Jesus Christ?

We can start with His title: "King of Salem." In Hebrew the word "salem" is "shalom" which means "peace." Just as "Jeru-salem" means "City of Peace." So, His title is "King of Peace" in Genesis 14:18-20:

> 18 **And <u>Melchizedek king of Salem</u> brought forth bread and wine: and he was the priest of the most high God. 19 And he blessed him, and said, Blessed be Abram of the most high God, possessor of heaven and earth: 20 And blessed be the most high God, which hath delivered thine enemies into thy hand. And he gave him tithes of all.**

Did you notice that Melchizedek "brought forth bread and wine " and blessed Abram who would later be called Abraham. In response, Abram gave him "tithes" or one-tenth of all the spoils he had. Later, under the Mosaic Covenant, all Jews would be required to give one-tenth to God each year.

In Psalms, we find the second reference to Melchizedek. King David records a dialog between the LORD, called Elohim, and David's Lord, called Adonai Who is Jesus Christ. Psalms 110:1-4:

> 1 **The LORD said unto my Lord,**
> **Sit thou at my right hand, until I make**
> **thine enemies thy footstool.**
>
> 2 **The LORD shall send the rod of thy**
> **strength out of Zion: rule thou in the**
> **midst of thine enemies.**
>
> 3 **Thy people shall be willing in the day**
> **of thy power, in the beauties of holiness**
> **from the womb of the morning: thou**
> **hast the dew of thy youth.**
>
> 4 **The LORD hath sworn, and will not**
> **repent [turn], Thou art a priest forever**
> **after the order of Melchizedek.**

Jesus was appointed by God to be a priest "after the order of Melchizedek" which is eternal. We see this appointment again in the book of Hebrews.

Now, having seen the verses to which the

following refers, we can continue with Hebrews 5:6:

6 As he saith also in another place, Thou art a priest forever after the order of Melchisedec.

Paul goes on to speak more about this Priest. In the following verses, think of Jesus Christ in the Garden of Gethsemane. There, he pleaded three times, ". . . saying, O my Father, if it be possible, let this cup pass from me: nevertheless not as I will, but as thou wilt" (Matt. 26:39). We see it again in Matthew 26:42-44. Yet, in spite of His fear, He remained faithful to the Father's will! Verses 7-8:

7 Who in the days of his flesh, when he had offered up prayers and supplications with strong crying and tears unto him that [Who] was able to save him from death, and was heard in that he feared;

8 <u>Though he were a Son, yet learned he obedience by the things which he suffered;</u>

Jesus Christ, both a Man and a Jew, had faith. He proved it by His actions of obeying the Father's will.

In His life on earth, Jesus Christ was both Man and Devine. He obeyed God with provable faith and He fulfilled the Law. By accomplishing this, Christ was made perfect before God. His resurrection is proof of God's acceptance. The following verse specifically applies to the Jews. Why? Because their eternal salvation is contingent upon them having faith to obey God's instruction. Verse 9:

9 **And being made perfect, he became the author of eternal salvation unto all them that obey him;**

The Jews are required to obey the Law. At His Ascension, Jesus instructed His Apostles. We find this at the end of Matthew. Verses 28:19-20:

19 **Go ye therefore, and teach all nations, baptizing them in the name of the Father, and of the Son, and of the Holy Ghost:**

20 **Teaching them to observe all things whatsoever I have commanded you: and, lo, I am with you alway, even unto the end of the world. Amen.**

Jesus Christ was called by His Father to be High Priest of the order of Melchisedec. Versed 10-11:

10 Called of God an high priest after the order of Melchisedec.

11 Of whom we have many things to say, and hard to be uttered, seeing ye are dull of hearing.

It appears that some of the Jews continued to be "dull of hearing." Paul doubts they will understand this.

During the Apostle Paul's ministry, he would first go the local synagogue. As a Pharisee, he was knowledgeable of the Scripture and able to teach. Here we see an example. Acts 17:1-3:

1 Now when they had passed through Amphipolis and Apollonia, they came to Thessalonica, where was a synagogue of the Jews: **2** And Paul, as his manner was, went in unto them, and three sabbath days reasoned with them out of the scriptures,

3 <u>Opening and alleging, that Christ must needs have suffered, and risen again from the dead; and that this Jesus, whom I preach unto you, is Christ.</u>

The word "Christ" comes from the Greek word

Christos meaning "Anointed One" or "Messiah."

As a teacher, Paul stated that those who received this letter should be teaching others, but instead, they need to be taught themselves. This he wrote out of concern and love for his brethren. Hebrews 5:12-13:

> **12 For when for [at] the time ye ought to be teachers, ye have need that one teach you again which be the first principles of the oracles of God; and are become such as have need of milk, and not of strong meat.**
>
> **13 For everyone that useth milk is unskilful in the word of righteousness: for he is a babe.**

He divides the Jews into two groups. Some are still babes who need the basics like milk. Others are mature in the faith and deserve meat. Paul provides them with meat. These others are capable of discerning between good and evil. Verse 14:

> **14 But strong meat belongeth to them that are of full age, even those who by reason of use have their senses exercised to discern both good and evil.**

6

Hebrews 6

Paul has laid the basic foundation for the Jews. Now, with that covered, he begins with the word "therefore" and moves beyond basic principles. Hebrews 6:1:

> 1 **Therefore leaving the principles of the doctrine of Christ, let us go on unto perfection; not laying again the foundation of repentance from dead works, and of faith toward God,**

The word "doctrine" means "teaching." He lists a few subjects he wants to teach them then adds "if God permit." Verses 2-3:

> 2 **Of the doctrine of baptisms, and of laying on of hands, and of resurrection**

of the dead, and of eternal judgment.

3 And this will we do, if God permit.

Paul is a man known for his love and compassion, but also for his bluntness when necessary. In this letter, he presents information these Jews need to know. You might ask, "Why?" Unlike those saved by grace through faith in believing the Gospel of Grace, those who are under the Gospel of the Kingdom will not be raptured. When Jesus said to the Twelve, "But he that shall endure unto the end, the same shall be saved" (Matt. 24:13), of what end was Jesus speaking?

Christ referred to the Tribulation. Like a refiner's fire, Jacob (true Israel) must be tested and endure to be saved. In Matthew 24, Jesus answered His disciples' question. Matthew 24:3:

> **3 And as he sat upon the mount of Olives, the disciples came unto him privately, Tell us, when shall these things be? and what shall be the sign of thy coming, and of the end of the world?**

It will be worth your time to read Matthew 24 as it provides valuable details about the end times.

From the following, it appears that those who once heard and accepted the Gospel of the Kingdom have turned away from it. These will have difficulty renewing their repentance. Paul states the reasons why. Hebrews 6:4-6:

> **4 For it is impossible for those who were once enlightened, and have tasted of the heavenly gift, and were made partakers of the Holy Ghost,**

> **5 And have tasted the good word of God, and the powers of the world to come,**

> **6 If they shall fall away, to renew them again unto repentance; seeing they crucify to themselves the Son of God afresh, and put him to an open shame.**

This was the subject of many of Jesus' parables. One such parable concerned seeds of wheat and the tares or weeds. It described how the harvest will occur during the Tribulation. (See Matt. 13:24-30.) Verses 7-8:

> **7 For the earth which drinketh in the rain that cometh oft upon it, and bringeth forth herbs meet [suitable] for**

them by whom it is dressed [prepared], receiveth blessing from God:

> 8 But that which beareth thorns and briers is rejected, and is nigh [near] unto cursing; whose end is to be burned.

During Noah's time, the global judgment was by flood. The coming judgment will be by fire.

Paul hoped that those to whom he was writing would not suffer this judgment. God sees their work as proof of their faith as they have ministered and continue to minister in His name. For those who do endure, there will be "things that accompany salvation." Verses 9-10:

> 9 But, beloved, we are persuaded better things of you, and things that accompany salvation, though we thus speak.

> 10 <u>For God is not unrighteous to forget your work and labour of love, which ye have shewed toward his name</u>, in that ye have ministered to the saints, and do [continue to] minister.

As they persevere in the faith, they show their commitment through works. Their diligence will keep them conscious of "the full assurance of hope" promised to them. He assures them that through works "through faith and patience" they will "inherit the promises." Verses 11-12:

> 11 **And we desire that every one of you do shew the same diligence to the full assurance of hope unto the end:**
>
> 12 **That ye be not slothful, but followers of them who through faith and patience inherit the promises.**

Promises are to be hoped for through faith in the One Who made those promise. Paul presents Abraham as an example to the Jews who held onto the promises God made to him. Verses 13-15:

> 13 **For when God made promise to Abraham, because he could swear by no greater, he sware by himself,**
>
> 14 **Saying, Surely blessing I will bless thee, and multiplying I will multiply thee.** 15 **And so, after he had patiently endured, he obtained the promise.**

God is always faithful to keep His promises. Verses 16-18:

> **16 For men verily swear by the greater: and an oath for confirmation is to them an end of all strife.**
>
> **17 Wherein God, willing more abundantly to shew unto the heirs of promise the immutability [unchangeable nature] of his counsel, confirmed it by an oath:**
>
> **18 That by two immutable [unchangeable] things, in which it was impossible for God to lie, we might have a strong consolation, who have fled for refuge to lay hold upon the hope set before us:**

It is against God's nature to change either Who He is or what He has said. That makes it impossible for Him to lie. All who follow Him can take consolation in knowing what God has said will not change. Furthermore, what God has promised will surely come to pass. We have His Word on that!

In changing and troubling times, those who have received promises from God can "anchor" their minds by faith in the One Who promised. The Jews' hope for the future and the fulfillment of those promises made are secure. They have as their High Priest in the heavenly Temple One Who continually intercedes on their behalf. Verses 19-20:

> 19 **Which hope we have as an anchor of the soul, both sure and stedfast, and which entereth into that within the veil;**

> 20 **Whither the forerunner is for us entered, even Jesus, made an high priest for ever after the order of Melchisedec.**

Unlike the men who served as High Priest in the Levitical priesthood, their current High Priest is "after the order of Melchizedek. He is their eternal High Priest.

7

Hebrews 7

Paul begins by returning to Melchisedec in Hebrews 7:1-2:

> 1 **For this Melchisedec, king of Salem, priest of the most high God, who met Abraham returning from the slaughter of the kings, and blessed him;**
>
> 2 **To whom also Abraham gave a tenth part of all; first being by interpretation King of righteousness, and after that also King of Salem, which is, King of peace;**

Consider the following comparison in verse 3:

> 3 **Without father, without mother, without descent, having neither begin-**

**ning of days, nor end of life; but made
like unto the Son of God; [Who] abideth
a priest continually.**

Since this occurred prior to the birth of Jesus Christ,
we are talking about a pre-incarnate state as Jesus
would later have a human mother. This is similar to
God walking in the cool of the day in the Garden of
Eden. Regardless, I believe that Melchisedec was
indeed Jesus Christ, the Son of God, appearing in the
flesh.

He continues in verses 4-5:

**4 Now consider how great this man was,
unto whom even the patriarch Abraham
gave the tenth of the spoils.**

**5 And verily they that are of the sons of
Levi, who receive the office of the
priesthood, have a commandment to
take tithes of [from] the people
according to the law, that is, of their
brethren, though they come [also came]
out of the loins of Abraham:**

Although Jesus Christ was born of the seed of
Abraham as His earthly father, He was also the Son
of God. Verses 6-10:

6 But he whose descent is not counted from them received tithes of [from] Abraham, and blessed him that had the promises.

7 And without all contradiction the less [lesser] is blessed of [by] the better. 8 And here men that die receive tithes; but there he receiveth them, of whom it is witnessed that he liveth.

9 And as I may so say, Levi also, who receiveth tithes, payed [paid] tithes [while] in Abraham. 10 For he was yet [still] in the loins of his father, when Melchisedec met him.

Paul puts forth a question for consideration. If perfection or salvation comes through the priests or the Law, both being received from Moses, then what need is there for another priest? Verses 11-13:

11 If therefore perfection were by the Levitical priesthood, (for under it the people received the law,) what further need was there that another priest should rise after the order of Melchisedec, and not be called after the order of Aaron?

12 For the priesthood being changed, there is made of necessity a change also of the law.

13 For he of whom these things are spoken pertaineth to another tribe, of which no man gave attendance at the altar.

The Levites were the only ones who had the honor of serving at the altar under Moses. Yet, Christ was born from the tribe of Judah and there is no mention about any descendants from Judah serving.

Christ did not meet the requirements to be a member of the Levitical priesthood. Verse 14:

14 For it is evident that our Lord sprang out of Juda; of which tribe Moses spake nothing concerning priesthood.

In the next verse, the meaning of the word "similitude" is best understood as "likeness" or "image." Verses 15-17:

15 And it is yet far more evident: for that after the similitude [likeness] of Melchisedec there ariseth another priest,

16 Who is made, not after the law of a carnal commandment, but after the power of an endless life.

17 For he [God] testifieth, Thou art a priest for ever after the order of Melchisedec.

It was God Who proclaimed to His Son, "Thou art a priest forever after the order of Melchizedek" (Ps. 110:4). Christ's appointment to this priesthood was by divine authority.

We see the word "commandments" and think of the Ten Commandments. These are just a portion of the Mosaic Law. Salvation can never be obtained by the Law. The Law was only a schoolmaster. (See Gal. 3:21-25.) The purpose of the Law was to teach the Jews they need to be dependent upon God. Verses 18-19:

18 For there is verily a disannulling of the commandment going before for the weakness and unprofitableness thereof. **19** For the law made nothing perfect, but the bringing in of a better hope did; by the which we draw nigh unto God.

Only judgment and condemnation come from the Law, but hope came through Jesus Christ.

Paul explained the purpose of the Law to the Gentiles in Romans 3:19-20:

> 19 **Now we know that what things soever the law saith, <u>it saith to them who are under the law</u>: that every mouth may be stopped, <u>and all the world may become guilty before God</u>.** 20 **<u>Therefore by the deeds of the law there shall no flesh be justified in his sight: for by the law is the knowledge of sin.</u>**

Think about this. If there is no speed limit, there is no law broken for speeding. However, if there is such as law and it is posted. Then, by breaking that law also comes judgment and a penalty that did not previously exist. Keeping all of the Law proved to be impossible. The Law was to make sinners dependent on God. The priesthood provided a temporary "covering" for their sins.

Christ became High Priest not by men. He received His appointment directly from God. Hebrews 7:20-21:

> 20 **And inasmuch as not without an oath**

he was made priest:

21 (For those priests were made without an oath; but this with an oath by him that said unto him, The Lord sware [swore] and will not repent, <u>Thou art a priest for ever after the order of Melchisedec:</u>)

This method of appointment and the order of priesthood to which Christ was appointed made a strategic difference. Verse 22:

22 By so much was Jesus made a surety of a better testament.

The word "surety" means "guaranty." What would be the basis of this guaranty? It would be a better testament or, in another word, covenant! This may raise a few eyebrows and it can be better explained.

Think about this. When something better comes along, whatever is better is also different than what it was before. Do you remember when we looked at a new covenant that God would make with the house of Judah and the house of Israel? (You can find it in Jer. 31:31-32.) Wait until you see this! The Jews were ones who knew their Scriptures since they had been taught it from an early age. At the Last

Supper on the night before He was crucified, Jesus was with His disciples. Here are His words. Matthew 26:26-28:

> 26 **And as they were eating, Jesus took bread, and blessed it, and brake it, and gave it to the disciples, and said, Take, eat; this is my body.**
>
> 27 **And he took the cup, and gave thanks, and gave it to them, saying, Drink ye all of it;** 28 <u>**For this is my blood of the new testament, which is shed for many for the remission of sins.**</u>

There were no questions asked as they were familiar with Jeremiah's prophecy. Can you see that the words "testament" and "covenant" are used interchangeably? A covenant requires that blood and sacrifice be involved. Here, the blood and sacrifice belong to the Lamb of God.

In Hebrews 8, Paul is going to go into greater detail to explain the significance. There is one important point I need to bring to your attention. For those who are familiar with the Gospel of Grace, you know that salvation is by grace through faith in that gospel. Immediately upon believing, salvation is different. It is received as a gift. The key words being "is received." However, this is not the case under the Gospel of the Kingdom. Here, the key word is "remission." Here, the word "remission" is not the same as "forgiveness." In this New Covenant, the blood of Christ provides temporary cover for the "remission" of sins until He returns. We saw this previously. For those who "shall endure unto the end, the same shall be saved" (Matt. 24:13). In other words, Israel will receive their salvation at the end of the Tribulation when He returns for them.

We find the same applies to baptism as well. When the Apostle Peter finished speaking to the crowd at the Pentecost Festival, they were convicted. Look at Peter's answer to their question. Acts 2:37-39:

> 37 **Now when they heard this, they were pricked in their heart, and said unto Peter and to the rest of the apostles, <u>Men and brethren, what shall we do?</u>**
>
> 38 **Then Peter said unto them, <u>Repent, and be baptized every one of you in the name of Jesus Christ for the remission of sins</u>, and ye shall receive the gift of the Holy Ghost.**

39 <u>For the promise is unto you, and to your children</u>, and to all that are afar off, even as many as the Lord our God shall call.

Here, again, is the word "remission." It places their sins in remission until they are forgiven at the Second Coming. There will be more to come about this in Hebrews 8. It is best to wait until then when we will discuss it further.

Paul discusses the Levitical priests in order to compare the priesthood of Jesus Christ. Hebrews 7:23-25:

23 And they truly were many priests, because they were not suffered to continue by reason of death:

24 But this man [Jesus Christ], because he continueth ever, hath an unchangeable priesthood.

25 Wherefore he is able also to save them to the uttermost that come unto God by him, seeing he ever [forever] liveth to make intercession for them.

The eternal nature of their High Priest Who serves

God in the heavenly and eternal Temple is far superior. The Levitical priests were, at best, only temporary because they were human and died.

Their High Priest once experienced what the Jews themselves are now experiencing. He understands this and has compassion for them. Never having sinned, He is able to intercede for them forever. Here, the word "became" has the meaning of "in general, to suit or be suitable, to be congruous or to befit; to be in accord with, in character or circumstances; to be worthy." This definition is from www.av1611.com. Jesus Christ is "worthy, suitable, or befitting" as High Priest. Verses 26-27:

> 26 **For such an high priest became us, who is holy, harmless, undefiled, separate from sinners, and made higher than the heavens;**
>
> 27 <u>**Who needeth not daily, as those high priests, to offer up sacrifice, first for his own sins, and then for the people's: for this he did once, when he offered up himself**</u>.

Jesus Christ is different from the men who served as High Priest. They were frail and sinful men. Daily they sacrificed for their sins and the sins of the people. However, Jesus Christ sacrificed only once when He offered Himself as the sacrifice for His brethren.

The Father appointed His Son as High Priest by speaking it. He would be the High Priest over Israel forever. Verse 28:

> 28 **For the law maketh men high priests which have infirmity; but the word of the oath, which was since the law, maketh the Son, who is consecrated for evermore.**

8

Hebrews 8

Paul has reached a point in this letter where he feels it is necessary to summarize for them what he has said thus far. Hebrews 8:1-2:

> 1 **Now of the things which we have spoken [thus far] this is the sum: We have such an high priest, who is set on the right hand of the throne of the Majesty in the heavens; 2 A minister of the sanctuary, and of the true tabernacle, which the Lord pitched, and not man.**

Paul is alluding to the tabernacle in the Wilderness which was like pitching a tent. It was a type or representation of the Temple in heaven. The tabernacle in the Wilderness was constructed according to God's instructions. It was a temporary dwelling for God. The true tabernacle is in heaven along with its sanctuary. It is within this sanctuary that Jesus Christ intercedes for them as their High Priest.

The priests who served God in the earthly Temple in Jerusalem where merely a shadow representing the heavenly One to come. Verses 3-5:

> 3 **For every high priest is ordained to offer gifts and sacrifices: wherefore it is of necessity that this man have somewhat also to offer.**
>
> 4 **For if he were on earth, he should not be a priest, seeing that there are priests that offer gifts according to the law:**
>
> 5 **Who serve unto the example and shadow of heavenly things, as Moses was admonished of God when he was about to make the tabernacle: for, See, saith he, that thou make all things according to the pattern shewed to thee in [upon] the mount.**

On Mount Sinai, God gave Moses specific instructions concerning the construction of the tabernacle which must be followed. Moses did as

God requested. It was an exact representation of what was to come.

In other letters, Paul used these two words "but now" to contrast what "was" in the past to what is "now" in effect. He does this below when discussing the New Covenant which he calls "a better covenant." (See Jer. 31:31-32.) This new covenant with the house of Judah and the house of Israel became effective on the night before Jesus was crucified. While enjoyed His last meal with His disciples, He introduced this covenant. Luke 22:19-20:

> 19 **And he took bread, and gave thanks, and brake it, and gave unto them, saying, This is my body which is given for you: this do in remembrance of me.**
>
> 20 **Likewise also the cup after supper, saying, This cup is the new testament in my blood, which is shed for you.**

His Twelve who were present at this meal were representatives of the Kingdon Jews – true Israel.

With the above in mind, we can move on to Hebrews 8:6:

6 But now hath he [Jesus Christ] obtained a more excellent ministry, by how much also he is the mediator of a better covenant, which was established upon better promises.

The first covenant was established through Moses. Israel became a protectorate state under the Sovereign King. The covenant made between them is sometimes referred to as a Suzerain-Vassal Covenant. As such, it did not allow for negotiation between the two parties. It was presented to Israel and they had the choice to accept or reject it.

The Vassal is a weaker nation that was saved by a powerful king. God saved Israel from Pharoah! They could never have achieved this on their own. Also, while in the Wilderness, Israel remained completely dependent upon God for provisions and protection. The key word here is "dependent." When God, the powerful Suzerain, presented a covenant agreement to Israel, they accepted the terms. They were contractually bound! This was the Mosaic Covenant.

In this covenant were certain terms that were included. These are often referred to as "the blessings and curses." Contractually, if Israel obeyed "all" of the specified requirements, then God would bless them. However,. if Israel failed to obeyed "all" of the specified requirements, then God would curse them. James reminded the remnant of this latter provision in their agreement. James 2:10:

> 10 **For whosoever shall keep the whole law, and yet offend in one point, he is guilty of all.**

We discussed God's purpose for Mosaic Covenant previously. The Mosaic Law was intended to be a schoolmaster to teach Israel dependence upon their God. He knew that Israel was head-strong and high-minded. Paul explains the purpose of the Law in Galatians 3:21-25:

> 21 **Is the law then against the promises of God? God forbid: for if there had been a law given which could have given life, verily righteousness should have been by the law.**

> 22 **But the scripture hath concluded all under sin, that the promise by faith of Jesus Christ might be given to them that believe.**

> 23 **But before faith came, we were kept under the law, shut up unto the faith**

which should afterwards be revealed.

24 Wherefore the law was our schoolmaster to bring us unto Christ, that we might be justified by faith. 25 But after that faith is come, we are no longer under a schoolmaster.

The only weakness with the Law was intentional. No one could live up to all its strict requirements except God. I will add that the Levitical priesthood was initiated with the Mosaic Law. Yet, all they could do was cover over the sins of Israel. Remission is only covering the sin, not eradicating it. That will happen in the future. Like all men, Israel remained prideful and they must be humbled. Israel will eventually acknowledge their dependency upon their Creator.

As we continue with Hebrews, you have seen these verses from Jeremiah before. Their importance makes them worth reading again. Hebrews 8:7-9:

7 For if that first covenant had been faultless, then should no place have been sought for the second.

8 For finding fault with them, he saith, Behold, the days come, saith the Lord,

80

**when I will make a new covenant with
the house of Israel and with the house
of Judah:**

**9 Not according to the covenant that I
made with their fathers in the day <u>when
I took them by the hand to lead them
out of the land of Egypt;</u> because <u>they
continued not in my covenant, and I
regarded them not,</u> saith the Lord.**

The Old Testament is replete with stories of Israel's
failures to keep the Law and, by doing so, they had
lost their faith in Who God was to them.

When we read Scripture and God is using the
future tense such as "I will" or "I shall," then we
know that it is prophecy. The text we have been
reading from Jeremiah is going to present a prophecy
still to come. Its fulfillment refers to the end times.[2]
Verses 10-12:

**10 For this is the covenant that <u>I will
make</u> with the house of Israel after
those days, saith the Lord; I will put my**

---

[2] All the promises and prophecies that God made to Israel
will be fulfilled at the end of the Tribulation. This is dealt
with at length in my book, *The Glorious Destiny Of Israel*.

laws into their mind, and write them in their hearts: and I will be to them a God, and they shall be to me a people:

11 And they shall not teach every man his neighbour, and every man his brother, saying, Know the Lord: for [because] all shall know me, from the least to the greatest.

12 <u>For I will be merciful to their unrighteousness, and their sins and their iniquities will I remember no more.</u>

The last verse recalls the prophecy given to Israel by Jeremiah. It refers to the completion of the Tribulation. Jeremiah 31:34:

34 And they shall teach no more every man his neighbour, and every man his brother, saying, Know the LORD: for they shall all know me, from the least of them unto <u>the greatest of them, saith the LORD: for I will forgive their iniquity, and I will remember their sin no more.</u>

The Old Covenant is superseded but not negated by the New Covenant. Nothing has changed, but a promise has been added. God never changes His Word. However, He can meet the requirements of the Old Covenant Himself. This He did through His Son. The New Covenant is through His Son's blood. And, as High Priest, He is able to intercede on behalf of His people Israel. Verse 13:

> 13 In that he saith, A new covenant, he hath made the first old. Now that which decayeth and waxeth [grown] old is ready to vanish away.

God said, "I will put my laws into their mind, and write them in their hearts." Therefore, He has not changed the Law,! He has fulfilled the Law on behalf of Israel. All they must do is believe, show proof of their faith, and endure to the end.

9

Hebrews 9

In the Wilderness at the base of Mount Sinai , Israel became a holy nation unto God. The word "holy' does not mean "perfect," it means "separated." God is holy, therefore Israel is to be separated from the world like God. Their role as God's people began right there. God desired to dwell with His people and gave instruction to Moses to create a tabernacle. The word "tabernacle" means "dwelling" if it is used a noun, but if used as a verb it can mean "to dwell." The tabernacle was a "type" or representation of the Temple. God gave strict rules or "ordinances" for its operation by priest appointed to that task.

Paul goes into detail describing this tabernacle in the Wilderness. It is recorded in Exodus 25-31, 35-40, and 39-40. We start with Hebrews 9:1-5:

1 Then verily the first covenant had also ordinances of divine service, and a worldly sanctuary.

2 For there was a tabernacle made; the first, wherein was the candlestick, and the table, and the shewbread; which is called the sanctuary.

3 And after the second veil, the tabernacle which is called the Holiest of all;

4 Which had the golden censer, and the ark of the covenant overlaid round about with gold, wherein was the golden pot that had manna, and Aaron's rod that budded, and the tables of the covenant;

5 And over it the cherubims of glory shadowing the mercyseat; of which we cannot now speak particularly.

Within this temporary structure, God would "dwell" or "tabernacle" with His people Israel.

The Mosaic Covenant included establishing the Levitical priesthood. Aaron became the first High

Priest. His descendants would continue that tradition. Today, many who have the last name of Levi or Cohen are part of that lineage. The inner most part of the tabernacle contained the Ark of the Covenant which was the symbol of Israel's special relationship with God. The Holy of Holies was only accessible to the High Priest once a year – only on the Day of Atonement. The mercy seat of God was in this inner sanctuary. Verses 6-7:

> 6 Now when these things were thus ordained, the priests went always into the first tabernacle, accomplishing the service of God.

> 7 But into the second went the high priest alone once every year, not without blood, which he offered for himself, and for the errors of the people:

It is evident that when God established the Mosaic Covenant, He anticipated that there would be failure on the part of His people. For that reason, the priesthood was established. It continued until the destruction of the Temple in A.D. 70.

The service of these Levitical priest was limited due to their own human frailty. Verses 8-10:

8 The Holy Ghost this signifying, that the way into the holiest of all was not yet made manifest [known], while as the first tabernacle was yet standing:

9 Which was a figure [type] for the time then present, in which were offered both gifts and sacrifices, that could not make him that did the service perfect, as pertaining to the conscience;

10 Which stood only in meats and drinks, and divers washings, and carnal ordinances, imposed on them until the time of reformation.

The word "reformation" would be the comparable to the "restoration" both referring to the time of the promised Kingdom.

Jesus Christ serves as High Priest in the tabernacle in heaven – a tabernacle not made by hands. Paul makes a comparison between the old priests and the new, Jesus Christ. Verses 11-13:

11 But Christ being come an high priest of good things to come, by a greater and more perfect tabernacle, not made with hands, that is to say, not of this build-

ing;

12 Neither by the blood of goats and calves, but by his own blood he entered in once into the holy place, having obtained eternal redemption for us.

13 For if the blood of bulls and of goats, and the ashes of an heifer sprinkling the unclean, sanctifieth to the purifying of the flesh:

Christ's sacrifice is far superior to those regular sacrifices made by ordinary men serving God. Verse 14:

14 How much more shall <u>the blood of Christ</u>, who through the eternal Spirit offered himself without spot to God, purge your conscience from dead works to serve the living God?

A priest is one who stands between a holy God and sinful people. As a prophet brings the words of God to the people, a priest brings the requests of the people to God. A priest acts as a mediator. Verse 15:

15 And for this cause he is the mediator of the new testament, that by means of

death, for <u>the redemption of the</u> <u>transgressions that were under the first</u> <u>testament [old covenant]</u>, they which are called might receive <u>the promise of</u> <u>eternal inheritance</u>.

They could not attain salvation under the old covenant. However, those who are faithful might receive salvation under the new covenant – the promise of eternal inheritance.

The following is going to get into the legality of a testament. You have no doubt heard the words "last will and testament." This document cannot become effective until the death of the "testator." This is the person to whom the last will and testament applies. Verses 16-17:

> 16 **For where a testament is, there must also of necessity be the death of the testator.**
>
> 17 **For a testament is of [in] force after men are dead: otherwise it is of no strength at all while the testator liveth.**

Every testament becomes effective upon a death. Paul explains that the first testament, or Mosaic Covenant required death or blood to become valid. Verses 18-21:

> 18 **Whereupon neither the first test-ament was dedicated without blood.** 19 **For when Moses had spoken every precept to all the people according to the law, he took the blood of calves and of goats, with water, and scarlet wool, and hyssop, and sprinkled both the book, and all the people,**
>
> 20 **Saying, <u>This is the blood of the testament which God hath enjoined unto you</u>.** 21 **Moreover he sprinkled with blood both the tabernacle, and all the vessels of the ministry.**

The Mosaic Covenant was a testament that became effective by the death or blood from the sacrifice of animals. This was a "type" or foreshadowing of the coming sacrifice of God's Son. The tabernacle and everything associated with it were sprinkled with blood to consecrate it.

Under the Law, which is the Mosaic Covenant, everything was to be purged with blood by sprinkling. The word "purged" means "purified or cleansed." Therefore, to separate anything that is unpure or sinful from God, blood is the only remedy.

Blood is obtained by the taking of a life because life is in the blood. However, the blood of animals only provided for temporary "remission." Remission comes from the Latin word "remissio" which means "to send back." All this would only provide a temporary covering to be dealt with permanently in the future. Verse 22:

> **22 And almost all things are by the law purged with blood; and without shedding of blood is no remission.**

The things of the earthly tabernacle were copies or patterns of the heavenly which is far superior. Verses 23-24:

> **23 It was therefore necessary that the patterns of things in the heavens should be purified with these; but the heavenly things themselves with better sacrifices than these.**
>
> **24 For Christ is not entered into the holy places made with hands, which are the figures of the true; but into heaven itself, now to appear in the presence of God for us:**

The true tabernacle in heaven was not made by

hands and this is the one where Jesus Christ enters on behalf of Israel.

Paul now compares the earthly priests to Jesus Christ the High Priest of the heavenly tabernacle. He comes from a different and more superior priesthood and His personal righteousness surpasses His earthly predecessors. Verse 25:

> 25 **Nor yet that he should offer himself often, as the high priest entereth into the holy place every year with blood of others;**

As High Priest, Jesus does not need to offer himself as a sacrifice repeatedly – once was sufficient for all Through the singular sacrifice of His Son, God will restore His Creation and put an end to sin. Verse 26:

> 26 **For then must he often have suffered since the foundation of the world: <u>but now once in the end of the world hath he appeared to put away sin by the sacrifice of himself</u>.**

God knew before the beginning that Creation would fail. He knew that Israel would fail and reject their Messiah. Everything in the restoration of Creation is by the works or actions of God.

Consider Peter's speech to Israel at Pentecost. Acts 2:22-24:

> **22 <u>Ye men of Israel</u>, hear these words; Jesus of Nazareth, a man approved of God among you by miracles and wonders and signs, which God did by him in the midst of you, as ye yourselves also know:**
>
> **23 Him, <u>being delivered by the determinate counsel and foreknowledge of God</u>, ye have taken, and by wicked hands have crucified and slain:**
>
> **24 <u>Whom God hath raised up</u>, having loosed the pains of death: because it was not possible that he should be holden of it.**

God knew everything that would happened in advance and planned His Solution. God spared not His Own Son Who is the Solution!

We must not fall into dispensational misinterpretation as many churches do today. The book of Hebrews was sent to Jewish believers – true Israel. They are the ones who hold to the promises of the Kingdom Gospel. They believe that Jesus Christ is their Messiah and the Son of God. They keep the Law and demonstrate their faith by doing good works. All this they do to achieve their salvation and they must endure to the end.

The wages or consequence of sin is death. All have sinned and, therefore, all must suffer death. This applies to both Jews and Gentiles. The following verse is used to proof there is no second chances. Once someone dies, there is the judgment. Hebrews 9:27:

> 27 **And as it is appointed unto men once to die, but after this the judgment:**

There is no reincarnation or multiple lives as some man-made religions teach. Prior to death, God offers a solution and people have a choice. There is the Gospel of Grace offered through the Apostle Paul and there is the Gospel of the Kingdom offered by the Twelve.

In this last verse, Paul refers to the Second Coming of Jesus Christ. This must not be confused with the Rapture when Christ appears in the clouds and calls to Himself those saved by grace through faith. They will have been removed prior to the Tribulation. The Second Coming occurs at the end of the Tribulation. The pronoun "them" in verse 28 can

95

only refer to faithful Israel who look with hope to His return. Verse 28:

> 28 **So Christ was once offered to bear the sins of many; and <u>unto them that look for him shall he appear the second time without sin unto salvation</u>.**

Those who are the faithful and have endured to the end, He will save. He will save true Israel and will forgive their sins forever. Jesus Christ, a Son of David, will become King over the eternal Kingdom promised to King David. He will reign in righteousness forever.

10

Hebrews 10

The Law was not a mistake. In fact, the Law was perfect. Anyone who was able to follow the Law complete would be perfect. Think about that for a moment. As mentioned before, the Law was intended to be a schoolmaster and, as such, it served its purpose well. It proved that all would sin and fall short of the perfection or glory of God. Even with the sacrifices, God would need to provide the Jews with another way. What was needed, He did Himself. Hebrews 10:1

> 1 <u>For the law</u> having a shadow of good things to come, and not the very image of the things, <u>can never</u> [even] with those sacrifices which they offered year by year continually <u>make the comers thereunto perfect.</u>

The Law along with its sacrificial rites could only provide a temporary remission or putting aside of sin. It could not "take away" sin.

The sacrifices made by the regular priests only covered their sins. They could not make them perfect before God. Had they made them perfect, there would have been no need for the sacrifices to continue. Verses 2-4:

> 2 **For then would they not have ceased to be offered? because that the worshippers once purged [made pure] should have had no more conscience of sins.**
>
> 3 **But in those sacrifices there is a remembrance again made of sins every year.**
>
> 4 **For** <u>**it is not possible that the blood of bulls and of goats should take away sins**</u>**.**

When Christ returns, His sacrifice, once applied, will be sufficient for Israel's sins to be "taken away" and remembered no more.

In Psalms, the Hebrew book of praise, there are

many references to their coming Messiah. The following provides us with an understanding of the relationship between the Father and Son. Here, the Son is speaking to the Father. Psalms 40:6-8:

> **6 Sacrifice and offering thou didst not desire; mine ears hast thou opened: burnt offering and sin offering hast thou not required.**

> **7 Then said I, Lo, I come: in the volume of the book it is written of me,**

> **8 I delight to do thy will, O my God: yea, thy law is within my heart.**

Jesus Christ knew that what pleased God and what He desired most. It is to do God's will and have His Law written in the heart.

Paul uses the above verses to show that Christ understood God's true desire. Hebrews 10:5-7:

> **5 Wherefore when he cometh into the world, he saith, Sacrifice and offering thou wouldest [desireth] not, but a body hast thou prepared me:**

> **6 In burnt offerings and sacrifices for**

sin thou hast had no pleasure. 7 Then said I, Lo, I come (in the volume of the book it is written of me,) to do thy will, O God.

Like any father, it appears that God desires obedience. It is truly an acknowledgement of Who His is.

He continues by pointing out that God does not desire the offerings for sin according to the Law. He does not delight in the sins that these offerings temporarily cover. Sin is disobedience and contrary of the desire of God. Verse 8:

8 Above when he said, Sacrifice and offering and burnt offerings and offering for sin thou wouldest [desireth] not, neither hadst pleasure therein; <u>which are offered by the law</u>;

Although the Law required the sacrifices, they were not pleasing to God. The sacrifices did nothing more than abate the stench of sin.

To remedy this, Christ took it upon Himself to please God. Verses 9-10:

9 Then said he, Lo, I come to do thy will,

O God. He taketh away the first [old covenant], that he may establish the second [new covenant].

10 By the which [latter] will we are sanctified through the offering of the body of Jesus Christ once for all.

Here are the two covenants to which Paul is referring. First, there is the Mosaic Covenant by which no one could obtain salvation – for the Law can only condemn. God gave a new covenant to the house of Israel and the house of Judah. (See Jer. 31:31-32.) This new or second covenant makes salvation or the "taking away" of sins possible!

The earthly priests continually served God by making the same sacrifices day after day. Verse 11:

11 And every priest standeth daily ministering and offering oftentimes the same sacrifices, which can never take away sins:

These priests were inferior to the High Priest. Why is that? Jesus Christ, the High Priest in heaven, made only one sacrifice – Himself! Verse 12:

12 But this man, after he had offered one

sacrifice for sins forever, sat down on the right hand of God;

In Psalms 110, God said to His Son, "... Sit thou at my right hand, until I make thine enemies thy footstool" (Ps. 110:1). Paul mentions this elevated position of Christ in verses 13-14:

13 From henceforth expecting till [until] his enemies be made his footstool.

14 <u>For by one offering he hath perfected forever them that are sanctified</u>.

He refers to the "one offering" or singular sacrifice made by Jesus Christ as being sufficient forever. However, it applies only to those who are "sanctified" which means "separated or set a part" from the world and from unbelief.

The Holy Spirit is the silent Witness to all that God has done, is going, and will do. It was the Spirit Who inspired the words of the Prophet Jeremiah who is quoted here by Paul. Verses 15- 18:

15 Whereof the Holy Ghost also is a witness to us: for after that he had said before, 16 <u>This is the covenant that I will make with them after those days</u>, saith

the Lord, <u>I will put my laws into their</u> <u>hearts, and in their minds will I write</u> <u>them;</u>

17 And <u>their sins and iniquities will I</u> <u>remember no more</u>. 18 Now where remission of these is, <u>there is no more</u> <u>offering for sin</u>.

This continues to be the main theme here. Under the old covenant, sacrifices only covered the sins of the Jews and placed them in remission. However, the new covenant will eradicate sin and, as a result, "there is no more offering for sin."

This puts the faithful Jews in a completely different position. Yes, they are still under the Law. However, they are no longer bent under its weight. They have Jesus Christ Who is both their High Priest and Messiah. Previously, we discussed the three offices of the Messiah. They were Prophet, Priest, and King. Presently, we see the Messiah in His second office as Priest. The faithful Jews can now enter the Holy of Holies with confidence because of the blood of Jesus. Verses 19-20:

19 Having <u>therefore, brethren, boldness</u> <u>to enter into the holiest</u> by the blood of Jesus, 20 By a new and living way, which

he hath consecrated for us, through the veil, that is to say, his flesh;

He chose the words "a new and living way" to describe the new covenant. He does this because the sacrifice for the new covenant is living. Yes, Jesus Christ is the living sacrifice. No one would enter behind the veil that separated the holy of holies. But now, the faithful can draw near to God through Christ.

True Israel can draw near for another reason. Out of a sincere heart, they hold onto the hope of what is to come. They have the "full assurance of faith" having their consciences consecrated by the blood and their bodies washed in baptism. Verses 21-22:

> 21 **And having an high priest over the house of God;** 22 **Let us draw near with a true heart in full assurance of faith, having our hearts sprinkled from an evil conscience, and our bodies washed** with **pure water.**

These Kingdom Believers were instructed to repent and be baptized. The word "repent" means "to change one's mind or direction." God wants the believer to turn from their sinful ways and turn back to God. It is an about-face. It generally includes a public profession or statement of faith. Following this, the Kingdom believer is baptized as a symbol of the cleaning done within.

Paul encourages these believers not to change after making their profession. This is easier if those of like-mind encourage each other. They must never forget, they must hold onto their faith, and they must "endure to the end." Verses 23-24:

> **23 Let us hold fast the profession of our faith without wavering; (for he is faithful that promised;) 24 And let us consider one another to provoke unto love and to good works:**

The word "provoke" means "to excite or move to action." This is something that every Kingdom Believer is encouraged to do. They must hold onto their faith – their hope – while encouraging others to love and do good works as proof of their faith.

The Jewish people have always been people of community. For them, they maintained close bonds with others of like mind. Verse 25:

> **25 Not forsaking the assembling of ourselves together, as the manner of some**

is; but exhorting one another: and so much the more, as ye see the day approaching.

He mentioned "the day approaching" which is a reference to the coming Tribulation. During this time all of Israel will be tested to determine who is true Israel. Faithful Jews are well aware of this. As this time approaches, they should continue to gather to encourage and exhort each other.

Throughout the Old Testament, Israel continued to lose their faith and sin against God. Under the new covenant, God requires proof they are maintaining their faith until the end. Paul warns those who abandon that faith that there is no other alternative sacrifice available to them. Having believed once, having failed there is no other option. Remember, this letter is written to Kingdom Believers. Do not misapply this dispensationally as it cannot be applied to those saved by grace through faith. Verses 26-27:

> 26 **For if we sin wilfully after that we have received the knowledge of the truth, there remaineth no more sacrifice for sins, 27 But a certain fearful looking for of judgment and fiery indignation, which shall devour the adversaries.**

Paul now compares Jews who committed sin under the old covenant with those Jewish believers who commits sin under the new covenant. This is especially offensive for those who now benefit from "the blood" of the new covenant. Verse 28:

> **28 He that despised Moses' law died without mercy under two or three witnesses:**

The above was the old covenant and the following is the new. Verse 29:

> **29 Of <u>how much sorer punishment</u>, suppose ye, <u>shall he be thought worthy, who hath trodden under foot the Son of God</u>, and hath counted the blood of the covenant, wherewith he was sanctified, an unholy thing, and hath done despite unto the Spirit of grace?**

Knowing the cost to purchase their salvation under the new covenant, what shall God think of those who minimize that gracious mercy?.

Paul warns Israel to fear and respect God Who has done for them all that is necessary to purchase their redemption. Verses 30-31:

30 For we know him that hath said, Vengeance belongeth unto me, I will recompense, saith the Lord. And again, <u>The Lord shall judge his people.</u>

31 It is a fearful thing to fall into the hands of the living God.

Many who converted to the Kingdom Gospel heard and believed the good news not long ago. Then, there arose a great persecution which caused great suffering for these new believers.

He recalls those events for them. Verses 32-33:

32 But call to remembrance the former days, in which, after ye were illuminated, ye endured a great fight of afflictions; **33** Partly, whilst ye were made a gazingstock both by reproaches and afflictions; and partly, whilst ye became companions of them that were so used.

A "gazingstock" is a form of punishment where many were made public spectacles. Its purpose was to intimidate others by showing them what awaited others who chose to follow.

Paul often referred to his own ministry as "my bonds." It appears that some of these Jews were kind to him during his own afflictions. These believers aided him because they thought less of their earthly goods than the treasures stored for them in heaven. Verse 34:

34 For ye had compassion of me in my bonds, and took joyfully the spoiling of your goods, knowing in yourselves that ye have in heaven a better and an enduring substance.

This brought Paul to his next point. Trials and tribulations often shake a believer's faith. Being aware of this, he encouraged them to remain confident in their promised reward. They must hold fast to the promises and hope of their salvation. The word "recompense" means "repayment, compensation, or benefit." It is the hope of that benefit than makes this worth their while. That benefit is their future salvation. Verses 35-36:

35 Cast not away therefore your confidence, which hath great recompence of reward. 36 For ye have need of patience, that, after ye have done the will of God, ye might receive the promise.

They must remain patient, continue to do their Father's will while they wait to receive His promise.

He tells them that not-to-far-away is the day which the Messiah will return for them as promised. This is the threshing floor. This is the refiner's fire. The period of testing will come. Verses 37-38:

> 37 **For yet a little while, and he that shall come will come, and will not tarry.**
>
> 38 **Now the just shall live by faith: but if any man draw back, my soul shall have no pleasure in him.**

They must press on. They must not draw back in doubt of receiving their benefit! Verse 39:

> 39 **But we are not of them who draw back unto perdition; but of them that believe to the saving of the soul.**

This is the nature of the Kingdom Gospel and it relates to Kingdom Believers only. Those who draw back are called "back-sliders." They believe but later change their minds. However, faithful believers, or true Israel, must continue in their faith. Their actions are the *proof* of their faith before God and other Jews and they *must* endure to the end!

11

Hebrews 11

Faith is believing. We are not talking about blind faith as faith must have an object to which we attach that faith. Faith in the Bible is believing or trusting in what God has said. This applies to both the Gospel of Grace and the Gospel of the Kingdom. The Jews have a history of failing faith, so God requires them to continually prove their faith by actions or works. This was not always the case. In fact, it was the faith of their fathers that brought them to the point of being the favored nation of God. Paul uses the word "elders" to include the "fathers" of the Hebrew faith. This current chapter, Hebrews 11, is often referred to as Faith's Hall of Fame.

Paul begins by defining faith. Hebrews 11:1-2:

1 Now faith is the substance of things

hoped for, the evidence of things not seen. 2 For by it the elders obtained a good report.

It was "by faith" the elders obtained a "good report." This means they received approval from God because they believed Him. They trusted what He told them. It is by faith that we understand how Creation came to be. Without faith in God's Word, our ability to explain our existence is reduced to scientific theory. However, by believing God's Word, we know the truth. Verse 3:

3 Through faith we understand that the worlds were framed by the word of God, so that things which are seen were not made of things which do appear.

Paul takes his readers on an historic journey through Israel's illustrious history. He writes about the great men of faith who heard God and believed Him. I have captioned these example as he works through a list. Paul will draw a conclusion from these examples in verses 4-12:

Abel and Cain:

4 By faith Abel offered unto God a more excellent sacrifice than Cain, by which

he obtained witness that he was righteous, God testifying of his gifts: and by it he being dead yet speaketh.

Enoch:

5 By faith Enoch was translated that he should not see death; and was not found, because God had translated him: for before his translation he had this testimony, that he pleased God.

6 <u>But without faith it is impossible to please him: for he that cometh to God must believe that he is, and that he is a rewarder of them that diligently seek him.</u>

Noah:

7 <u>By faith</u> Noah, being warned of God of things not seen as yet, moved with fear, prepared an ark to the saving of his house; by the which he condemned the world, and became heir of the righteousness which is by faith.

Abraham:

8 <u>By faith</u> Abraham, when he was called to go out into a place which he should after receive for an inheritance, obeyed; and he went out, not knowing whither he went.

9 <u>By faith</u> he sojourned in the land of promise, as in a strange country, dwelling in tabernacles with Isaac and Jacob, the heirs with him of the same promise: 10 For he looked for a city which hath foundations, whose builder and maker is God.

Sarah:

11 <u>Through faith</u> also Sara herself received strength to conceive seed, and was delivered of a child when she was past age, because <u>she judged him faithful who had promised.</u>

12 Therefore sprang there even of one, and him as good as dead, so many as the stars of the sky in multitude, and as the sand which is by the seashore innumerable.

Paul draws a conclusion from these examples. His

purpose is to encourage the Jewish believers to hold fast to their faith even though that which has been promised has not yet happened. God is faithful. They need to have faith in Him. They must continue to believe God that will fulfill His Word. Their eternal salvation depends upon it. Verse 13:

> 13 **These all died in faith, not having received the promises, but having seen them afar off, and were persuaded of them, and embraced them, and confessed that they were strangers and pilgrims on the earth.**

The Kingdom promised to the Jews is theirs. Presently, they are sojourners in a foreign land until they are called to return to the Promised Land. Then, God will make it their land as He promised their fathers.

Their hope is that they will possess the Promised Land. This land was promised to Abraham. Genesis 12:7:

> 7 **And the LORD appeared unto Abram, and said, Unto thy seed will I give this land** . . .

Here the word "seed" is singular. It refers to Abraham's greatest Son, Jesus Christ. Israel still hold onto the hope to possess the land promised to Abraham's *Seed*. And, they will when the Seed, their Messiah Jesus Christ, returns. Verses 14-16:

> 14 **For they that say such things declare plainly that they seek a country.**
>
> 15 **And truly, if they had been mindful of that country from whence they came out, they might have had opportunity to have returned.**
>
> 16 **But now they desire a better country, that is, an heavenly: wherefore God is not ashamed to be called their God: for <u>he hath prepared for them a city</u>.**

The City of Jerusalem is the beloved city of the Jews. God will fulfill His promise, they will possess the land. They will dwell in the New Jerusalem which God has prepared for them. He will personalize just for them! We find the fulfillment of God's promise in the book of Revelation.

The Apostle John recorded what he saw in heaven. Revelation 21:10-12:

> 10 **And he [the angel] carried me away in**

the spirit to a great and high mountain, and shewed me that great city, the holy Jerusalem, descending out of heaven from God,

11 Having the glory of God: and her light was like unto a stone most precious, even like a jasper stone, clear as crystal;

12 And [it] had a wall great and high, and had twelve gates, and at the gates twelve angels, and names written thereon, which are the names of the twelve tribes of the children of Israel:

Each of the twelve gates to the city will have a name from the twelve tribes of Israel! They will dwell (or tabernacle) with God forever.

Paul continues with this Faith Hall of Fame by providing further examples. Verses 17-31:

Abraham and Isaac:

17 By faith Abraham, when he was tried, offered up Isaac: and he that had received the promises offered up his only begotten son, 18 Of whom it was

117

said, That in Isaac shall <u>thy seed</u> be called: 19 Accounting that God was able to raise him up, even from the dead; from whence also he received him in a figure.

Jacob:

20 <u>By faith</u> Isaac blessed Jacob and Esau concerning things to come. 21 <u>By faith</u> Jacob, when he was a dying, blessed both the sons of Joseph; and worshipped, leaning upon the top of his staff.

Jospeh:

22 <u>By faith</u> Joseph, when he died, made mention of the departing of the children of Israel; and gave commandment concerning his bones.

Moses:

23 <u>By faith</u> Moses, when he was born, was hid three months of his parents, because they saw he was a proper child; and they were not afraid of the king's commandment.

24 <u>By faith</u> Moses, when he was come to years, refused to be called the son of Pharaoh's daughter;

25 Choosing rather to suffer affliction with the people of God, than to enjoy the pleasures of sin for a season;

26 Esteeming the reproach of Christ greater riches than the treasures in Egypt: for he had respect unto the recompence of the reward.

27 <u>By faith</u> he forsook Egypt, not fearing the wrath of the king: for he endured, as seeing him who is invisible.

28 <u>Through faith</u> he kept the passover, and the sprinkling of blood, lest he that destroyed the firstborn should touch them.

The Twelve Tribes:

29 <u>By faith</u> they passed through the Red sea as by dry land: which the Egyptians assaying to do were drowned.

30 <u>By faith</u> the walls of Jericho fell

down, after they were compassed about seven days. 31 By faith the harlot Rahab perished not with them that believed not, when she had received the spies with peace.

There are others in the Old Testament who provide us with more examples of great faith. Verses 32-38:

32 And what shall I more say? for the time would fail me to tell of Gedeon, and of Barak, and of Samson, and of Jephthae; of David also, and Samuel, and of the prophets:

33 Who through faith subdued king-doms, wrought righteousness, obtained promises, stopped the mouths of lions,

34 Quenched the violence of fire, escaped the edge of the sword, out of weakness were made strong, waxed valiant in fight, turned to flight the armies of the aliens.

35 Women received their dead raised to life again: and others were tortured, not accepting deliverance; that they might

obtain a better resurrection:

36 **And others had trial of cruel mockings and scourgings, yea, moreover of bonds and imprisonment:**

37 **They were stoned, they were sawn asunder, were tempted, were slain with the sword: they wandered about in sheepskins and goatskins; being destitute, afflicted, tormented;**

38 **(Of whom the world was not worthy:) they wandered in deserts, and in mountains, and in dens and caves of the earth.**

The point Paul is making is very poignant. Referring to these great people of faith, he said, "of whom the world was not worthy."

At the close of this chapter, we see a familiar phrase again: "having obtained a good report through faith." It was because they had faith in God's Word, they received a "good report." They were accepted. They were approved by God because of their faith. However, in spite of having received God's approval, they still did not receive the promise. Verses 39-40:

39 And these all, having obtained a good report through faith, received not the promise:

40 God having provided some better thing for us, that they without us should not be made perfect.

None of these witnesses had received their promised salvation. God is waiting for a reason. Paul explains this to his readers who are also waiting in faith for their salvation. If we read the last verse again, we will see why. It says that they will receive their salvation beside all these great witnesses of faith. They will receive salvation together. God provided something better for these current believers. Their holy predecessors were not made perfect by salvation . . . without them. Therefore, all of true Israel will be made perfect together. They are God's holy nation. All this will be accomplished by the Anointed One, Jesus Christ.

12

Hebrews 12

In his letter to the Jews, Paul presented them with numerous examples of the great faith of their elders. He refers to them as "a great cloud of witnesses." Perhaps they can picture them looking on as witnesses do, cheering them on. Knowing that the Tribulation is coming, Paul urges these believers to put aside their earthly cares and concerns. They must press on – regardless of their situation. Like the cloud of witnesses, they must hold onto their faith! Hebrews 12:1:

> 1 **Wherefore seeing we also are <u>compassed about with so great a cloud of witnesses</u>, let us lay aside every weight, and the sin which doth so easily beset us, and let us run with patience the race that is set before us,**

They have the perfect example to follow: Jesus Christ. He is "the Author and Finisher of their faith!" Verse 2:

> **2 Looking unto Jesus the author and finisher of our faith; who for the joy that was set before him <u>endured</u> the cross, despising the shame, and is set down at the right hand of the throne of God.**

All they need to do is consider what Christ endured to gain what was promised to Him. Verses 3-4:

> **3 For consider him that <u>endured</u> such contradiction [opposition] of sinners against himself, lest ye be wearied and faint in your minds.**
>
> **4 Ye have not yet resisted unto blood, striving against sin.**

Since they are alive, they have not resisted until death as Jesus Christ did Who willingly spilled His blood for them.

Out of love for them, the Lord disciplines His children. The word "chasten" means "to scold." The word "scourge" means "to punish usually by causing physical pain." Like a parent, God seeks to teach or instruct Israel. They are His children and He is their Father. As such, He diligently teaches them. Verses 5-6:

> 5 **And ye have forgotten the exhortation which speaketh unto you as unto children, My son, despise not thou the chastening of the Lord, nor faint when thou art rebuked of him:**
>
> 6 **For whom the Lord loveth he chasteneth, and scourgeth every son whom he receiveth.**

He teaches only those who are His sons or children. Verses 7-8:

> 7 **If ye endure chastening, God dealeth with you as with sons; for what son is he whom the father chasteneth not?**
>
> 8 **But if ye be without chastisement, whereof all are partakers, then are ye bastards, and not sons.**

For a father does not chastise or scold children who are not his own. Paul compares human fathers who correct their children and teach respect. If they listened to their earthly fathers, how much more should the Jews listen to their heavenly Father Who teaches them? Verse 9:

> 9 **Furthermore we have had fathers of our flesh which corrected us, and we gave them reverence: shall we not much rather be in subjection unto the Father of spirits, and live?**

Human fathers may discipline according to their whim. However, their heavenly Father seeks to prepare them for their future. Verse 10:

> 10 **For they verily for a few days chastened us after their own pleasure; but he [God] for our profit, that we might be partakers of his holiness.**

Being corrected by God is never pleasant. However, the benefits are "the peaceable fruit of righteousness" for those who learn their lesson. Verse 11:

> 11 **Now no chastening for the present seemeth to be joyous, but grievous: nevertheless afterward it yieldeth the peaceable fruit of righteousness unto**

them which are exercised thereby.

Many times our lives are filled with trials and tribulations that sap our strength and vigor. However, believers must straighten up and walk the straight and narrow path. "Straight" ways typically refer to "righteous" ways. Since the four Gospels were also written to Kingdom believers, look at this quote from Jesus. Matthew 7:13-14

> 13 **Enter ye in at the <u>strait gate</u>: for wide is the gate, and broad is the way, that leadeth to destruction, and many there be which go in thereat: 14 Because <u>strait is the gate, and narrow is the way, which leadeth unto life</u>, and few there be that find it.**

Paul continues with Hebrews 12:12-13:

> 12 **Wherefore lift up the hands which hang down, and the feeble knees; 13 And <u>make straight paths for your feet</u>, lest that which is lame be turned out of the way; but let it rather be healed.**

The phrase "lifting up the hands" usually means they should praise God. While "feeble knees" means that they are not "standing strong." They are to praise God, regardless of their situation standing strong and unwavering in their hope.

They are to lead the straight and narrow path of righteousness. Nothing has changed for the Jews. Look at what was written in Solomon's day. Proverbs 4:26-27:

> 26 **Ponder the path of thy feet, and <u>let all thy ways be established</u>.** 27 **Turn not to the right hand nor to the left: remove thy foot from evil.**

Jews always have the Law that was to establish all their ways. They should never turn to the right or to the left. They must continue on the straight path set before them by God. How are the Jews to interact with others? Paul continues his directions. Verses 14-15:

> 14 **Follow peace with all men, and holiness [separateness], without which no man shall see the Lord:**

> 15 **Looking diligently lest any man fail of the grace of God; lest any root of bitterness springing up trouble you, and thereby many be defiled;**

Isaac who was the son of Abraham had two sons: Esau and Jacob. Esau was the oldest. As the eldest son he possessed the birthright. However, he did not value his birthright and foolishly sold it to his brother for a bowl of stew. Here is the story that Jews knew all too well. Genesis 25:30-33:

30 And Esau said to Jacob, Feed me, I pray thee, with that same red pottage; for I am faint: therefore was his name called Edom.

31 And Jacob said, Sell me this day thy birthright. 32 And Esau said, Behold, I am at the point to die: and <u>what profit shall this birthright do to me</u>?

33 And Jacob said, Swear to me this day; and he sware unto him: <u>and he sold his birthright unto Jacob</u>.

Esau did not consider his birthright of any value when he was starving. Paul warns the Jews, regardless of their circumstances, to never do this! Hebrews 12:16-17:

16 Lest there be any fornicator, or profane person, as Esau, <u>who for one morsel of meat sold his birthright</u>.

17 For ye know how that afterward, when he would have inherited the blessing, he was rejected: for he found no place of repentance, though he sought it carefully with tears.

Later, there was no way for Esau to "repent" or "change his mind." The word "carefully" means Esau was "full of care" having heavy regret for his hasty decision. The Gospel of the Kingdom provides a means of salvation. However, the Jews are still under the Law which is their heritage. It is their "birthright."

Paul recall an event in the Wilderness when the Jews were camped at the base of Mount Sinai. Moses met face to face with God on the mountain and received the Law. Verses 18-21:

18 For ye are not come unto the mount that might be touched, and that burned with fire, nor unto blackness, and darkness, and tempest, 19 And the sound of a trumpet, and the voice of words; which voice they that heard intreated that the word should not be spoken to them anymore:

20 (For they could not endure that which

was commanded, And if so much as a beast touch the mountain, it shall be stoned, or thrust through with a dart: 21 And so terrible was the sight, that Moses said, I exceedingly fear and quake:)

In view of this terrible sight, the Jews and even Moses shook with fear.

Paul says that they are at a similar point in history again. God has brought the faithful Jews here once more. They are in the Wilderness today. He wants them to see where God has brought them, to see the great value in this, and not to forsake or despise their birthright as did Esau. Verse 22:

22 But ye are come unto mount Sion, and unto the city of the living God, the heavenly Jerusalem, and to an innumerable company of angels,

In the next verse, there are two words I would like to clarify. The word "church" means "the called-out ones." Out of all the nations, God "called out" the Jews as a special people for Himself. Both the English words "church" and "assembly" come from the same Greek word, EKKLESIA, which means "the called-out ones." Jesus Christ is the "firstborn" because He was the first to be raised from the dead. (Here we are talking about permanent resurrections and not resuscitations as in the Gospel miracles.) God's Son is the firstborn from the dead. Verses 23-24:

> 23 To the general assembly and church of the firstborn, which are written in heaven, and to God the Judge of all, and to the spirits of just men made perfect,
>
> 24 And to Jesus the mediator of the new covenant, and to the blood of sprinkling, that speaketh better things than that of Abel.

Cain and Abel were the first two children of Adam and Eve. Abel was a shepherd while Cain farmed the land. God accepted Abel's sacrifice, but Cain's He did not. In a fit of rage, Cain killed Abel. This is another story all Jews know. Abel obeyed God and his sacrifice was accepted by God. Cain did as he pleased and his sacrifice was not accepted.

Paul focuses their attention on Jesus Christ their Mediator. Those who refused to listen to Him on earth could not escape the consequences of their choice. How much more will those who refuse to listen to Him speak to them today from heaven. He is speaking about the words of their apostles and letters sent to them inspired by God. This is the purpose of Hebrews, the seven Hebrew Epistles, and Revelation. True Israel was not left uninformed! Verse 25:

> **25 See that ye refuse not him [Jesus Christ] that speaketh. For if they escaped not who refused him that spake on earth, much more shall not we escape, if we turn away from him that speaketh from heaven:**

Paul seeks to instill fear to respect the words of instruction God has given them.

Paul now turns to the future with the great judgment to come. Verse 26:

> **26 Whose voice then shook the earth: but now he hath promised, saying, Yet once more I shake not the earth only, but also heaven.**

At the base of Mount Sinai, the voice of God was heard by the children of Israel. Its sound shook the earth and they were frightened. Here, Paul tells them that this will happen again. However, this next time His voice will shake both earth and heaven. Speaking of things in Creation that were made, if they are shaken, then they will be removed. While that which is not shaken will remain. Verse 27:

> 27 And this [spoken] word, Yet once more, signifieth the removing of those things that are shaken, as of things that are made, that those things which cannot be shaken may remain.

This brings Paul to his conclusion on this matter. Creation can be shaken as can all things that are made. It is a shaking out of these things which will reveal those things which are worthy of God. What are those things?

God cannot be shaken and neither can His Kingdom. God promises that He will restore His Kingdom. The Jews are to hold to this promise made to King David. The faithful Jews who endure will have an important role to play in this coming Kingdom. This role is not for the weak of faith. God is preparing Israel. Verses 28-29:

> 28 Wherefore we [who are] receiving a kingdom which cannot be moved, let us have grace, whereby we may serve God acceptably with reverence and godly fear: 29 For our God is a consuming fire.

13

Hebrews 13

In the times to come, things will get difficult if not unbearable for the Jews. Following the Rapture, there will be seven years before the Messiah returns as their King. Until then, who can these believers turn to, if not each other? Hebrews and the seven Hebrew Epistles were written to them. They are to encourage and instruct these believers to endure to the end. In the Kingdom, the Jews will have the Law written on their hearts. They must observe what has been called the Golden Rule. Jesus taught this from His earthly ministry. Matthew 7:12:

> 12 **Therefore all things whatsoever ye would that men should do to you, do ye even so to them: for this is the law and the prophets**.

Paul wrote to the Romans, "Love worketh no ill to his neighbour: therefore love is the fulfilling of the law" (Rom. 13:10). Additionally, the act of showing love is evidence of keeping their faith!

With that said, let us begin the last chapter of Hebrews staring with verses 1-3:

> **1 Let brotherly love continue. 2 Be not forgetful to entertain strangers: for thereby some have entertained angels unawares.**
>
> **3 Remember them that are in bonds, as bound with them; and them which suffer adversity, as being yourselves also in the body.**

Faithful Jews must be ethical in their living. They are to exercise kindness and compassion as they too are in a human body. They should fear God and His judgement treating God and His Word with respect. Verses 4-6:

> **4 Marriage is honourable in all, and the bed undefiled: but whoremongers and adulterers God will judge.**
>
> **5 Let your conversation be without cov-**

etousness; and be content with such things as ye have: for he hath said, I will never leave thee, nor forsake thee.

6 So that we may boldly say, The Lord is my helper, and I will not fear what man shall do unto me.

They should be content with what they have and not desire things that others have. They know that they are not alone, that Christ is with them, They can be confident of this and, therefore, have no reason to fear.

In A.D. 70, the Jews rose up against Roman rule and they lost. Jerusalem was destroyed. The next great battle which will be fought against the enemies of the Jews will not be fought by them alone. At the very end of the Tribulation, when all hope appears to be lost, Jesus Christ will return. This time He will be acting in His third office as King of Israel. He will destroy all who seek to destroy Israel and establish His eternal Kingdom. Therefore, true Israel must hold onto the hope with full confidence in God, His promises, and His Son!

Paul continues in verse 7:

7 Remember them which have the rule

**over you, who have spoken unto you
the word of God: whose faith follow,
considering the end of their
conversation.**

Paul tells them that those who oversee their faith
were sent to them by God for a reason. The word
"conversation" means "manner of living or
lifestyle." As they approach the end times, they
should follow their examples concerning their
manner of living. Their leaders were sent to set an
example for them.

Many things have changed, are changing or
will change. Regardless of this, they must have
confidence in Jesus Christ Who will fulfill the
promises. Verse 8:

**8 Jesus Christ the same yesterday, and to
day, and for ever.**

I recommend that every believer read the entire
chapter of Matthew 24 as it specifically addresses the
end times. Matthew 24:11

**11 And many false prophets shall rise,
and shall deceive many.**

They must know what God has promised and not fall

for other strange teachings. Hebrews 13:9:

> 9 **Be not carried about with divers [various] and strange doctrines. For <u>it is a good thing that the heart be established</u> with grace; not with meats, which have not profited them that have been occupied therein.**

Paul compares the sacrifices (plural) made by the priests under the old covenant with the sacrifice (singular) made by Jesus Christ. He serves as their High Priest under the new covenant. Verses 10-11:

> 10 **We have an altar, whereof they [the priests] have no right to eat which serve the tabernacle.**

> 11 **For the bodies of those beasts, whose blood is brought into the sanctuary by the high priest for sin, are burned without [outside] the camp.**

Now, he compares this to Jesus. Verses 12-13:

> 12 **Wherefore Jesus also, that he might sanctify the people with his own blood, suffered without the gate.**

13 Let us go forth therefore unto him without [outside] the camp, bearing his reproach.

The Temple was located inside the City of Jerusalem. Yet, the faithful Jews look upon the Son of God Who was crucified outside the city.

Jerusalem was destroyed in A.D. 70., since then they waited having faith in God's promise for the City and Kingdom to come. Verses 14- 16:

14 For here have we no continuing city, but we seek one to come.

15 By him therefore let us offer the sacrifice of praise to God continually, that is, the fruit of our lips giving thanks to his name.

16 But to do good and to communicate forget not: for with such sacrifices God is well pleased.

No longer offering sacrifices at the Temple of God, they can do so now by giving God praise and thanksgiving from their lips. With hope of the promise to come, these are well-pleasing to God.

God has set over the people leaders to oversee them and their wellbeing. They should respect them as they are God's servants. Submit to them with joy and do not cause strife. Verse 17:

17 Obey them that have the rule over you, and submit yourselves: for they watch for your souls, as they that must give account, that they may do it with joy, and not with grief: for that is unprofitable for you.

Paul wrote this letter from Rome while being held for his trial before Caesar. He hoped to return to them. Verses 18-19:

18 Pray for us: for we trust we have a good conscience, in all things willing to live honestly.

19 But I beseech you the rather to do this, that I may be restored to you the sooner.

Throughout the four Gospels, Jesus is referred to as the Shepherd and Israel as the sheep. (In the Pauline epistles, those saved by grace through faith are never referred to as sheep.) When Jesus sent out His disciples to proclaim the Gospel of the Kingdon, He gave these instructions. Matthew 10:5-6:

5 These twelve Jesus sent forth, and commanded them, saying, Go not into the way of the Gentiles, and into any city of the Samaritans enter ye not: 6 But go rather to the lost sheep of the house of Israel.

With that, let us read to whom the New Covenant applies. Hebrews 13:20-21:

20 Now the God of peace, that brought again from the dead our Lord Jesus, that great shepherd of the sheep, through the blood of the everlasting covenant,

21 Make you perfect in every good work to do his will, working in you that which is well-pleasing in his sight, through Jesus Christ; to whom be glory for ever and ever. Amen.

Even with Jesus Christ as their eternal High Priest, the Jews must continue in faith, do good works as evidence of that faith, and endure to the end.

Paul apologizes for writing what may appear to be chastisement. That was not his intent. Although Paul is imprisoned, Timothy was still free to travel.

It is his hope that both he and Timothy may be able to visit them shortly. Verses 22-23:

22 And I beseech you, brethren, suffer the word of exhortation: for I have written a letter unto you in few words.

23 Know ye that our brother Timothy is set at liberty; with whom, if he come shortly, I will see you.

In the salutation, very similar to those written in Paul's other letters, we see evidence that he is writing this letter from Rome.

24 Salute all them that have the rule over you, and all the saints. They of Italy salute you.

The final verse may cause some of you to raise an eyebrow. Grace is not exclusive to those who follow the Gospel of Grace. Grace also applies to those saved by the Gospel of the Kingdom. The Jews' salvation is also by God's grace. Their works do not "earn" them their salvation. The difference is that God requires them, based upon their history, to have faith. They must prove it with good works as "evidence" of their faith. Furthermore, they must endure to the end. It is only through God's grace that their salvation is possible! Verse 25:

25 Grace be with you all. Amen.

Epilogue

A teacher must learn first what he or she is going to teach. I will always be a student of God's Word as I continue to learn more about the Word of God. I would like to share with you what I learned from writing this book.

I enjoyed writing this commentary on Hebrews. Here is a word of warning to Bible students everywhere. We must never forget that a commentary is not equal to the inspired Word of God. He alone has the authority and it is before Him all true students must bow. Every teacher and preacher of the Word is human and subject to error. This includes me. I have listened to numerous sermons and they can all be broken down into two categories: expository and topical. If you are a serious student of the Bible, you should learn the difference.

Some who teach and preach have an incredible God-given talent. Some of them use Scripture in a way I call "springboard preaching." The Bible is their springboard. They bounce on several verses from the Bible, then they go airborne. Then, they dive right into a shallow pool of personal opinion. Of course both they and their hearers will say that they "preach from the Bible." But, in truth, they promote their own customs, traditions, and vain philosophies of men." Paul warns of this in Colossians 2:8:

> 8 **Beware lest any man spoil you through <u>philosophy and vain deceit</u>, after the <u>tradition of men</u>, after the <u>rudiments of the world</u>, and not after Christ.**

I will leave that to you to consider how you were taught in the past. Now, you must see Scripture in a different light. You must see it rightly-divided. It is the only way the whole Bible makes sense.

Compare that topical approach to the approached used in this book. You have in your hands an example of expository teaching. We went verse-by-verse through the entire book of Hebrews from beginning to end. We looked to find its meaning "within its context." Its interpretation must be congruent with all of Scripture. In other words, it must be consistent with the entire Bible. We know that the Word of God cannot contradict itself. When we understand what God has said through His Word, we are blessed. Is this not each believer's goal?

So, how can we know if someone is interpreting the Bible correctly? Here is the answer: we must test it. Paul and Silas called the Bereans more "noble" because that is exactly what they did. Acts 17:11:

> 11 **These were more noble than those in Thessalonica, <u>in that they received the word with all readiness of mind, and searched the scriptures daily, whether those things were so</u>.**

In other words, they listened but later verified that what Paul preached was true. It was in agreement with the Scriptures!

The book of Hebrews is difficult to understand without applying the dispensational approach. Some call this "rightly dividing" the Word. It is the same thing. I hate to leave people with questions. There are two books published by GraceWord Publishing that explain the dispensational approach. This is a interpretive tool. They also show you how to apply it. The first is Letters To Theophilus – Are You Ready For The End Times? The other is The Glorious Destiny Of Israel – The Fulfillment of God's Promises and Prophecies to Israel. These two books will provide you with a detailed understanding of God's plans for both the Jews and the Gentiles. It will make reading the Bible much easier.

I would like thank you for taking the time to read this book and pray that you received a blessing from it.

Saved by grace,
Dr. David Alan Greene

Resources

Berean Bible Society
www.bereanbiblesociety.org

Grace Believers Bible Study
www.gracebelieversbiblestudy.com

Grace Bible Network
www.gracebiblenetwork.org

Grace Church Directory
https://gracechurches.wordpress.com

GraceWord Publishing, LLC
www.gracewordpublishing.com

Through the Bible With Les Feldick
www.lesfeldick.org

Other GraceWord Publications

Cartas A Teófilo
Efesios: Dispensacionalmente Considerado
El Evangelio Oculto: Una vez fue un misterio . . .

About The Author

Dr. David Alan Greene has over thirty-five years of experience as an insurance agent selling both property and casualty as well as life insurance. During his career, he taught and explained the content and meaning of policies to his clients. Now retired, he devotes much of his time to teaching the Bible.

He received his Bachelor of Theology, Master of Biblical Studies, and Ph.D. in Biblical Studies from Evangelical Theological Seminary where he holds the position of Dean of Graduate Studies. He also holds a Ph.D. in Christian Counseling. He has written numerous biblical commentaries and books on rightly dividing the Word of Truth.